THE GERMAN ARMY 1933-45

A COLLECTOR'S GUIDE TO THE
HISTORY AND UNIFORMS OF DAS HEER:

THE GERMAN ARMY 1933-45

CHRIS ELLIS

IAN ALLAN Publishing

First Published 1993

ISBN 0 7110 2193 7

Designed by Ian Allan Studio

Published by Ian Allan Publishing

an imprint of Ian Allan Ltd, Terminal House,
Station Approach, Shepperton, Surrey
TW17 8AS; and printed by Ian Allan Printing
Ltd, Coombelands House, Coombelands Lane,
Addlestone, Weybridge, Surrey KT15 1HY.

Front cover: Two soldiers in greatcoats pictured on
the Russian Front, late in 1941. They wear the
standard greatcoat with waistbelt from the personal
equipment. Note stick grenade carried in belt. The
nearest man wears the standard field grey leather
gloves with ribbed backs, and the furthest man
wears knitted dark grey gloves and also has a helmet
band for the affixing of camouflage foliage.

Back cover:
Deutsche Afrika Korps
Figures, left to right: Oberleutnant of Artillerie in full
issue tropical uniform with the lightweight forage
cap (Feldmütze); Obergefreiter (corporal) of
Infanterie in rolled-up shorts and tropical helmet
(Tropische Kopfbedeckung); Hauptfeldwebel
(sergeant-major) of Infanterie in long trousers and
tropical shirt with shoulder straps. Note the reed
green colour of newly issued lightweight tropical
tunics and helmet; they later faded under desert
conditions.

Top left: National emblem (Hoheitszeichen) for
tropical dress.

Top right: Afrika Korps formation sign as carried on
vehicles and noticeboards.

Bottom: Afrika Korps cuff title.

Contents

Introduction

Interest in the momentous events of World War 2 seems never to decrease, despite the fact that the 1939-45 period is beyond the memory of a great number of those who now study it. The greatest fascination is almost always reserved for the arms and achievements of the country that was instrumental in starting the war, but in 1945 decisively lost it — Germany. The power of Nazi Germany's fighting forces, at least in the earlier part of the war, was certainly awesome. Even today photographs and old newsreels featuring the military machine of the Nazi era makes a striking visual impact which stays in the mind. The imagery lingers on. For example, a stage director today looking for a sinister oppressive uniform, even beyond the context of World War 2, is likely to choose a German Third Reich-era style with its suggestion of power and oppression rather than the innocuous and uninspiring 'roly poly' British battledress.

By the same token the Third Reich era often confuses those who are unfamiliar with the intricacies of the Nazi political system and the many uniformed organisations that were either linked directly to it, or, like the armed forces, were strictly speaking outside politics but depended on the patronage of its political leaders. Descriptions like 'Nazi officer', 'Gestapo', 'SS officer' and 'Nazi soldier' tend to be applied to any picture of anyone who is obviously a uniformed person from the Third Reich period. This may be inherited from the World War 2 period itself, when newspapers tended to identify pictures in this way, the emotive word being 'Nazi'.

For anyone wanting more accurate identification than this it is necessary to resort to reference books. In this one the most important element of the German Third Reich fighting machine, the Army (Heer) is isolated from all the rest and all the most important uniform items are illustrated and described. It must be emphasised, however, that the inventory of material supplied to the Heer was very big, so some minor items are omitted and it is certainly not possible to illustrate all the tiny variations that existed, even of some of the commoner badges. Some variations are still being discovered, even today, by collectors. This is due to the many different contractors and their individual interpretations of the instructions and specifications, etc, made even more complicated by later shortages and substitutions.

Added to the descriptions of the uniforms and insignia are sections giving a concise historical background to show how the Army fitted into the Third Reich political system and the events of World War 2, plus a similar concise coverage of organisation and command. Such subjects as medals and side arms are mentioned briefly because of their connection to uniforms and insignia, but for more comprehensive coverage of these there are other reference books available.

The object of this book is to make the subject of German Army uniforms easy to follow and to that end German language terms have been kept to what is essential and are generally given in parentheses when items are first mentioned. A listing of key terms is given in the appendices. The emphasis in the book is on what was and is most commonly seen, for example through contemporary World War 2 histories and newsreels. Hence rarely seen or less important uniform variations are not included. For example, the tiny insignia variations for Army officials (Beamten) are quite complex and to include them would fill another section of the book. But, on the other hand such officials as bakery service inspectors and war economists do not appear in many campaign photographs or newsreels! Also the foreign volunteers who served under Army command and jurisdiction are not included for that is more properly a subject in its own right.

Chris Ellis
Kingston-on-Thames   May 1993

ACKNOWLEDGEMENTS

For assistance in the compilation of material for this book, thanks are due to R. J. Marrion, Peter Chamberlain, Shin Ueda, and Alan Kemp. Malcolm Fisher of Regimentals very kindly arranged photographic facilities for specific items from his stock — all the individual pieces shown in this book — and considerable help was also given by Regimentals' staff, notably Tony Bradley.

Line drawings are by R. J. Marrion, Alan Kemp, Shin Ueda, and the author.

The back cover artwork is by R. J. Marrion.

1. Historical Background

The powerful German Army that fought through World War 2 grew out of the events of 1918-19 that brought World War 1 to an end. During that conflict the Kaiser's Imperial Army had expanded to a vast size. Some 11 million men either volunteered for, or were conscripted into, the German army during the years of conflict. Of that number about six million became casualties. By 1918 the years of unrelenting trench warfare had made those men who had survived the carnage into lean, mean, and resourceful individuals. Young officers and NCOs, many of them replacing regulars who had died, gained vast experience. Among them were several of the men who were to become well-known names in World War 2, including Rommel and Guderian.

The quality of the Kaiser's army and its field commanders was well demonstrated by the effectiveness and determination of its final push on the Western Front in the spring and early summer of 1918. Considerable gains were made, but at the cost of another half-million casualties. The war of attrition finally caught up with the German High Command after this exhausting offensive, and there were no reserves or resources left with which to halt the massive Allied counter-offensive of August 1918 which finally sealed the fate of Germany. Escalating shortages of supplies and ammunition, plus looming problems in Germany itself (including declining civilian morale, industrial unrest and left-wing agitation) convinced the German Commander-in-Chief (C-in-C) Hindenburg and the Chief of General Staff Ludendorff, that they had reached the end of the road and could no longer sustain the military effort.

Early in October 1918 the Kaiser decided to negotiate for peace to bring the fighting to an end. This was a protracted process which led to the abdication of the Kaiser on 9 November 1918 and one of his last acts was to appoint Hindenburg as supreme commander of all German armed forces. An Armistice was finally agreed on 11 November 1918. Army morale, at least on the Western Front, remained remarkably high until the end. It was, in effect, an undefeated army, numbering at the time about three million men in the west (and another million on the much more confused Eastern Front). But the army had surrendered on foreign soil — in France and Belgium in the west — with its command structure and formations intact. No enemy had reached German soil. In fact, Hindenburg and Ludendorff did a skilful job in distancing themselves and the army from ignominy for the defeat, swinging all blame on to incompetent politicians at home. In this way they managed to retain their honour and reputations and both they, and other generals, were able to continue military or political careers in the years that followed.

There was no time for complacency, however. With the fall of the Kaiser, Germany was declared a Socialist Republic with the Social Democrat Party in the majority but under threat from Revolutionary Socialists and Communists who were trying to destabilise the government. The terms of the Armistice called for a quick repatriation of the German soldiers on the Western Front and this was achieved within about three weeks. But returning to a demoralised homeland with an unsteady and insecure government brought any good intentions to an end. Soldiers deserted in droves — they simply went home — without waiting for demobilisation or any further orders. Men returning from the Eastern Front did so in even greater disorder. The German Army virtually collapsed and the Revolutionary Socialists and Communists took advantage of the situation to try to seize power.

THE FREIKORPS

To counter this disarray an unofficial 'army' of peacekeepers came into being from December 1918, with the aim of protecting property, industry and local government from takeover by revolutionaries intent on turning Germany into a Bolshevik state. The Russian Revolution was only one year old and it had sparked off revolutionary ideas all over Europe. The unofficial units, virtually private armies, were called Freikorps and they were mostly formed by ex-officers or men of local influence. They recruited from old soldiers (most of whom were unemployed) and students. Right-wing activists were also members of the Freikorps and it was in the Bavarian Freikorps at Munich in 1919 that the German Workers' Party (later the National Socialist German Workers' Party — NDSAP, abbreviated to Nazi) had its origins. This led, in a few years, to a major upheaval in the course of German history and the advent of the Third Reich.

There were several serious uprisings in 1919, notably in Berlin and Munich, where Communists attempted to seize control of the state. In the absence of an effective army, the government and the Army High Command (Oberst Heeresleitung) were pleased to be able to call on the Freikorps to put down these insurrections. Early in 1919 they saw considerable action against the Communist groups, but there was little co-ordination and the Freikorps units themselves varied in quality from reasonably disciplined — when strong in ex-Army men — to what amounted to little more than armed thugs out for what they could get.

THE VERSAILLES TREATY

The socialist government of the newly-established German Federal Republic convened at Weimar in February 1919 and Hindenburg planned to form a new national army (Reichsheer) using the unofficial Freikorps units as a basis. A standing army of 300,000 was envisaged. However, the Versailles Treaty drawn up in May and June 1919 (the official peace treaty between Germany and the Allies) caused this objective to be greatly modified. The Versailles Treaty was harsh and humiliating. Vast reparations payments to the Allies were demanded. Severe restrictions were placed on the armed forces. The standing army was to be limited to 100,000, of whom only 4,000 were to be officers. Aircraft, tanks and heavy weapons were prohibited. At the same time the navy was to surrender all big ships and only coastal forces would be permitted. The Allies were to put occupying troops into the Rhineland area and further restrictions included closure of military academies and training schools, and abolition of the old General Staff systems.

Hindenburg and his senior generals found all this unacceptable and resigned within days. However, the Weimar government had no real choice but to accept the military terms of the treaty. So the President, Friedrich Ebert, appointed an able and experienced, but more junior general, Major-Gen Hans von Seekt, to reorganise the army within the terms of the treaty.

Seekt was an inspired choice. In the very difficult political circumstances of the time he effectively created a new Reichsheer from the somewhat anarchic shambles of the Freikorps and built up a most proficient military organisation in his period of command (1920-26). He was the true 'father' of the German Army that went to war in 1939, though his name has been largely overshadowed by those military commanders who inherited and expanded upon what he had started.

THE REICHSHEER

The new Reichsheer came formally into being in October 1919 when a new defence ministry, the Reichswehr, was set up. Under it came the Marineleitung (Navy Command) and the Heeresleitung (Army Command). The first C-in-C of the Reichsheer was Gen Reinhard with Seekt as what was, in effect, Chief of the General Staff. But, because a conventional general staff was not allowed by the treaty terms, he was called Head of the Army Office. Seekt also became the C-in-C in 1920 following an attempted putsch in Berlin by a powerful group of right-wing Freikorps units. This putsch failed but it caused the left-wing factions to rise up in the Ruhr in an attempt to seize power. To quell this the Reichsheer was ordered in and Seekt was given absolute command of the Reichsheer to do whatever was necessary to suppress the uprising.

Once in total command, General Seekt could mould the Reichsheer to make best use of the numbers allowed. The 100,000 men were organised into two Army Groups, each with seven infantry and three cavalry divisions.

Though popular legend has it that the German Army was not covertly expanded until the Nazi era, Seekt systematically flouted the treaty limitations right from the start as a way of making the best of his limited numbers and restricted range of arms. The limited size of the regular army was overcome by forming an additional arm of the police, the Landespolizei, charged with dealing with civil disturbances. A frontier police force was also formed, the Grenschutz Ost, to patrol the eastern border with Poland. Several other units were formed of similar type, the net effect being to put men into uniform beyond the treaty limits without technically breaching it because they were not soldiers. However, they did receive quasi-military training to suit them for their security roles. Some of the cavalry units were used as a cover for transport and motorised units, too. The Army Office (Heeresamt), acting unofficially as the General Staff, also had planners working on armoured and air warfare matters together with other subject areas that were not supposed to be covered. This was long before Hitler was ever in sight of power.

Seekt's early career had been in an elite Guards regiment with the pre-1914 Prussian Army prior to a high level staff career during the Great War. Therefore he brought traditional Prussian values to his command experience with the Reichsheer. He paid particular attention to the officer corps, and as there was an establishment of only 4,000 there was keen competition for appointments and only the best were chosen. Former officers of the prewar regular army formed the backbone of the corps, backed by the pick of the keenest of the postwar generation. In the case of these men, officer candidates had to serve four years in the ranks before being commissioned. The Reichsheer was an all-volunteer force and enlisted men signed-on for 12 years. Senior NCOs were given a high degree of responsibility and these factors made the German Army much less class-conscious than some other European armies, including the British. It was possible, for instance, for senior NCOs in some circumstances to take command levels in the field that in other armies would be the task of junior officers.

Though Seekt tried to keep the Reichsheer out of politics, the suspicion in the public mind was that the army had right-wing sympathies. They generally took a lenient view of Freikorps excesses but cracked down hard on left-wing agitation. Nonetheless, Seekt, with an eye on future expansion, was among those who persuaded the German government in 1922 to make a secret agreement with the Soviet Union whereby Germany built armament factories and other establishments on Russian soil in exchange for secret training facilities for German troops in Russia. The common cause behind this arrangement was the potential need to contain Poland with which both countries had borders.

DOMESTIC INSTABILITY

The year 1923 was a turning point in the history of the Weimar government, for on 8 November of that year, Adolf Hitler and his NDSAP supporters staged the notorious Beer Hall Putsch in Munich, the event which was the first to bring him to world notice. The aim was, no less, to overthrow the unstable Bavarian government and, if successful, to march on Berlin. It was an ambitious and totally illegal venture which was put down by the local police force because, significantly, the Reichsheer commander in Bavaria refused to get involved. Hitler was arrested, tried for treason and imprisoned. During his time in jail he wrote *Mein Kampf* which was virtually his manifesto for future National Socialist rule.

Earlier in the year government stability had been threatened when French and Belgian troops occupied the Ruhr area because Germany failed to keep up with reparation payments. Meanwhile inflation was soaring and unemployment was high. In mid-November 1923, for example, the price of a stamp for a postcard was 40,000 million marks at the high point of inflation. At that time the exchange rate was 4.2 billion marks to the US dollar. This was the era of the million mark note and a suitcase full of money for the most routine purchases. Soup kitchens and poverty were the lot of millions. The situation antagonised middle class and working class alike.

Something had to be done, and with the help of America the near worthless currency was reformed with a new 'Rentenmark' replacing one million million old marks. The Dawes Plan, of which this was part, also revised the harsh reparation terms of the Versailles Treaty. The 1924-29 period, as a result, saw prosperity return to Germany as investment from abroad followed the newly stabilised currency. With loans coming in, mainly from America, the economy picked up quickly. There was much new building, re-equipment of factories, and rationalisation of industry — which caused some unemployment — but in general there was a feeling of well-being.

Following the failed Beer Hall Putsch there were threats of Communist insurrection in Bavaria, Thuringia and Saxony, plus Polish insurgency in Silesia. A state of national emergency was declared by the government and Seekt was given full powers to deal with the situation. The Reichsheer moved against the Communists with great efficiency in complete contrast with the reluctance they showed against Hitler's forces.

Hindenburg, still respected as a great World War 1 military leader, became President of the Republic in 1925 following the sudden death of President Ebert. He was no admirer of Seekt whom he forced to resign in 1926 following some minor political indiscretions. Seekt had run the Reichsheer with a high degree of autonomy and under his command it had become virtually a 'State within a State' answering more to Seekt than the government. However, his departure opened the way for the Reichsheer command to be taken over by senior officers who were old colleagues or protégés of Hindenburg, who in turn took a personal interest in the Reichsheer as a result of his distinguished military career. Notable among the generals were Wilhelm Groener and Kurt von Schleicher who had both held senior staff and command posts during the war. By 1928 a clique of former World War 1 generals held all the senior army and defence ministry posts.

In 1929 the short-term prosperity resulting from the Dawes Plan started to evaporate. Delayed reparation payments had piled up and stood at 132,000 million gold marks, a sum virtually impossible to repay. Germany was set for a long period of financial hardship as things stood. Even the most favourable plan would have Germany repaying 2,000 million gold marks annually in reparations until 1988. The government was in disarray and the right-wing opposition sought to create more mischief. In September 1929 Hitler proposed in the Reichstag an inflammatory 'Law against the Enslavement of the German People' which, among other things, would ignore reparation payments.

Apart from the reparations problem, for much of the 1924-29 period foreign investment in the

Weimar Republic was in the form of short-term loans from America which would be recalled if the economic situation deteriorated. The Wall Street Crash of 24 October 1929 therefore ravaged the German economy again as the vast loans were called in. There were massive bankruptcies and huge job losses counted in millions but insufficient government funds to pay unemployment benefit on this scale. In these conditions Hitler's appeal to disillusioned voters made great progress. He had a great ability in his speeches to present problems and the answers to them clearly and simply. He articulated the thoughts and aspirations of many with an appeal for nationalism and work for all in a somewhat idealised well-ordered society, for which he demanded racial (ie Aryan) purity.

THE NAZIS IN POWER

The year 1930 was another turning point in German history. The Communists and NDSAP — now with a very big 'private army', the Sturmabteilung (SA) — were in a state of open warfare. Reichsheer sympathies were becoming more openly right-wing. There was a well-publicised scandal when several Reichsheer officers were court-martialled for openly supporting the NDSAP. The general election of 1930 saw the NDSAP win 148 seats, their largest inroad yet in the Reichstag (parliament) against the combined 220 seats of the Social Democrats and Communists. The Nazis were the largest single party and Hindenburg as the President held the balance of power. There followed a couple of years of political intrigue as the various interests jockeyed for power. Wilhelm Groener became Minister of the Interior as well as Defence Minister. Schleicher liaised with Hitler to better his position and that of the Reichsheer.

The next presidential election took place in 1932 and Hindenburg was re-elected. Hitler was one of several other candidates. Groener as Interior Minister used the re-affirmed confidence in Hindenburg as an opportunity to ban the SA which he saw as the main cause of political unrest. The ensuing row led to the resignations of Groener and the Chancellor (prime minister), Brünning. A right-wing politician, Franz von Papen, was appointed as the new Chancellor and he, in turn, made Schleicher the War Minister. Von Papen's position was weak and he was forced into a General Election in July 1932. This time the Nazi Party won the greatest number of seats.

By rights Adolf Hitler should now have become Chancellor, but Hindenburg, still wary of

Plate 1: *Assembling dummy tanks around a BMW Dixi car for training exercises in 1928. The men are in the basic Reichsheer service dress.*

right-wing rule, would not appoint him. This lead to an uneasy stalemate during which time Schleicher was appointed as a stop-gap Chancellor. He did not have the confidence of the Reichstag, however, and he resigned on 28 January 1933. This time Hitler became Chancellor in a coalition government with Von Papen as his deputy.

HITLER AS CHANCELLOR

Once in the key seat of government, Hitler was able to entrench his Nazi Party. Gen Werner von Blomberg of the Reichsheer, a Nazi supporter, became War Minister and he in turn ensured that all the key army posts went to Nazi sympathisers as new appointments became due. On 27 February 1933 the infamous Reichstag fire incident took place, now generally regarded as a Nazi plot to create an artificial crisis. It gave Hitler a sound excuse to outlaw the Communist Party and round-up its leaders. Sweeping extra legal powers were announced to deal with any left-wing dissent. He wooed the Reichsheer by promising expansion and an enhanced national status. The

Plate 2: *Gen von Blomberg (right) with the new Chancellor Hitler (left) and Vice-Chancellor von Papen in March 1933. Blomberg, head of the Reichswehr, wears a 1916 pattern helmet, riding boots and a frockcoat with cross-belt. Note the portapee on the sword handle.*

Plate 3: *President Hindenburg lies in state in August 1934, guarded by four Reichsheer officers. Note the Reichsheer tunic with diagonal lower pockets, cross-belts and brown leather gloves. The Hoheitsabzeichen breast emblem is being worn and the black armbands are for mourning. The officer on the left is wearing the 1918 pattern cavalry helmet with 'scalloped' cut-outs in the rim. The others wear the 1916 pattern helmet. Full medals are worn.*

Plate 4: *The Chancellory Guard presents arms for Hitler as he leaves for a diplomatic function soon after becoming Chancellor. Note the Reichsheer service tunic with diagonal lower pockets, the officer with sword and cross-belt and next to him the drummer with 'Swallow's Nest' wings.*

and the Reichsheer from the SA which had now grown to great size and power under its commander Ernst Röhm. Röhm had ideas of creating a new 'people's army' based around the SA and with the Reichsheer diluted or incorporated in a subservient position. This did not suit Hitler or the Reichsheer and, fearing take-over by Röhm, Hitler had him eliminated and the SA broken up and reduced by its rival party arm the SS (Schützstaffel) on the infamous 'Night of the Long Knives', 30 June 1934. Schleicher was among several other possible 'trouble makers' who lost their lives in the brutal episode.

Early in August of that year old President Hindenburg died and Hitler took supreme control of the state, styling himself Führer (leader), effectively combining the posts of Chancellor and President in one. He also made himself chief of the armed forces. More sweeping changes were made to put the Nazi Party in total control of the state. All official bodies, including the Reichsheer, now had to swear allegiance to the Führer rather than the Republic. The new Nazi-controlled state was styled the Third Reich and Hitler's extreme ideas of racial purity and social planning were put into effect. An early priority was the promised expansion of the armed forces, overtly rather than covertly. An initial move in 1934 was to increase the size of the Reichsheer to 21 divisions from its existing seven divisions. This was done by forming new infantry regiments from the third and/or training battalions of the existing regiments, then forming new battalions in place of those that had been re-designated. Manpower for the expansion came from volunteers — unemployment was still high — and by transferring some of the Landespolizei battalions to the army.

red/yellow/black national colours of the Weimar Republic were replaced by the old Imperial red/white/black colours to emphasise the German tradition of power in Europe. From February 1934 the Nazi Hoheitsabzeichen (the eagle and swastika emblem) was added to uniform insignia to show the link between the army and the party.

There was an immediate threat to both Hitler

MILITARY EXPANSION

The big expansion started in 1935. A major enactment at the start of the year was the 'Law for the Reconstruction of the National Defence Forces'. This introduced conscription for all men of military age from 16 March 1935 and, of course, it had a big effect in reducing the unemployment figures as did the ensuing expansion of the armaments industry to equip the greatly enlarged armed forces. The compulsory period of military service was one year, but from August 1936 this was increased to two years. The army was to be further expanded to 36 divisions, the Luftwaffe (air force) was officially founded, ignoring the Versailles restrictions, and the Kriegsmarine (navy) was also to be expanded to a fighting fleet with a new warship building programme.

Under the new law the armed forces collectively were to be called the Wehrmacht (defence force) and the Reichsheer (state army) was to be renamed Das Heer (the army) so that with the Luftwaffe and Kriegsmarine it formed part of the Wehrmacht. To command the army a full general staff and headquarters was set up, the Oberkommando des Heeres — OKH (army high command). The first commander of the Wehrmacht was Gen Bromberg and the first commander of Das Heer was Gen Fritsch.

PANZER DIVISIONS

A significant development in October 1935 was the establishment of three Panzer (armoured) Divisions. They took over the few cavalry and motorised units of the old Reichsheer and were given a strength (on paper) of a panzer brigade (two tank regiments) and a rifle brigade (two infantry regiments) per division, though it was some time before these strengths were actually reached. Gen Otto Lutz was the first commander of the tank forces and his senior staff officer was Heinz Guderian who had led the planning and tactical thinking behind the establishment of the first Wehrmacht armoured divisions.

Guderian had been working towards this for some years. At the instigation of Guderian, training in tank warfare had started in 1927 with push-along dummy canvas tanks. This was improved upon for 1928 exercises by cladding BMW Dixi cars (licence-built Austin Sevens) with tank-shaped wood and canvas bodies to give more realistic mobility. These were the famous 'cardboard tanks' of legend which were often cited by British commentators in the 1930s to prove that the Germans were not really serious about tank warfare. But in actual fact German tank development had started in a small way well before the Nazis came to power. While the dummy training tanks were being built, secret orders went to Rheinmetall, Krupp and Daimler-Benz in March 1927 for the construction of actual prototype tanks under the 'camouflage' descriptions of Grosstraktor (heavy tractor). A lighter tank, the Leichtertraktor, was also ordered, as well a some armoured car prototypes. This was all done in strictest confidence because tanks flouted the Versailles Treaty terms. The prototypes were delivered in 1928 and sent to a secret tank testing ground at Kazan in Russia where a tank training school had been set up under the terms of the German-Russian agreement that Seekt had negotiated a few years earlier.

No orders were placed for these prototype tanks, possibly due to the economic conditions of 1929. The delay was useful for by 1931 Guderian had become chief staff officer to the mobile force commander and had had time to study the more advanced British ideas for armoured warfare as postulated by Fuller, Liddell Hart and others, and effectively demonstrated by the Experimental Armoured Force of 1928 and its successors. Guderian drew up a plan for a 'model' armoured division for the Reichsheer equipped with fast light

and medium tanks. These emerged in the la 1930s as the PzKpfw II and III. Meanwhile a Ca den-Loyd tankette chassis was purchased fro Britain to study for evaluation as a possible g carrier or tractor. It was realised that this cou be modified and adapted quickly to produce light training tank. To disguise its purpose, ho ever, it was described on purchase as bei needed as an 'agricultural tractor'. As develope it became the Panzerkampfwagen (PzKpfw) I a was in service in 1934.

Motorised companies were formed from 19 onwards and the first three Panzer (armoure divisions with the new PzKpfw I were formed 1935. In 1938 two more Panzer divisions we formed and by the outbreak of war in 1939 mo of the old cavalry divisions had been motoris and turned into light divisions. Other branches the Heer expanded at comparable rates. Co scription allowed massive expansion, at least o paper, but the increase in numbers of divisio exceeded the supply of really experienced pe sonnel and some of the formations were at lo strength. The 'Anschluss' with Austria in 19 (whereby Austria was forcibly taken into th Greater Reich) added five more divisions to th Heer. There were 66 Landwehr (reserve) div sions and some Landespolizei units which we

Plate 5: *Army manoeuvres in September 1936: an infantry howitzer battery at Bad Nauhei. The men ar wearing the initial issue of the 1936 pattern service dress which lacked the dark bottle green facing material on the collar and shoulder straps. 'Exercise bands' are just visible on the helmets.*

5

fully militarised and added to Heer strength. Thus, at the outbreak of war in September 1939 there were 103 Heer divisions of all sorts but little more than one-third of these were really effective well-equipped fighting formations. The Heer was never so well equipped as the very good German propaganda machine made out. Impressive tank formations were pictured, as were panzergrenadiers with armoured half-tracks. But these were only with the first line regular Panzer divisions and even they were short of some equipment. More lowly infantry divisions were highly dependent on horse-drawn transport for gun teams, supply, ambulances, field kitchens and other logistic support — in contrast with the British Army, for instance, which by 1939 was virtually 100% mechanised, at least in Europe.

The annexation of Czechoslovakia in early 1939 gave an important bonus to the Heer in that Germany acquired all the Czech arms industry with several well equipped factories, such as Skoda, and a mass of good Czechoslovak tanks and guns. These were valuable in making up the shortfall in the equipment for the Heer panzer divisions and became available just in time for the Polish campaign of September 1939, and more importantly for the invasion in the West in May-June 1940. Some of the divisions, such as Rommel's famous 7th Panzer Division, were almost wholly equipped with ex-Czech tanks.

At manpower level the transition from the old Weimar Reichsheer to the Third Reich's Heer saw significant changes. The uniform was greatly improved and updated. Badges and decorations were improved and more were instituted. New flags and banners were introduced for all organisations, the Heer included, which incorporated the new national colours and the swastika.

THE ROAD TO WAR

The path to war had started in March 1936 when Hitler flexed his muscles and marched troops into the demilitarised Rhineland in defiance of treaty agreements. Neither France nor Britain who had jurisdiction of the area, took military action. The Spanish Civil War also started in 1936 (and dragged on until 1939) and Hitler supported Franco's Nationalist forces with aircraft and military equipment, some instructors, and a volunteer fighting force, the Condor Legion. Though mainly an air arm, this included a military element and the exercise was a good testing ground for German tanks and other weapons, and gave good combat experience which was later useful to the Wehrmacht. After the annexation of Austria in 1938, pressure was next put on Czechoslovakia for the largely German-speaking Sudetenland area to be ceded to Germany. Meanwhile Hitler had made himself Supreme Com-

Plate 6: *Spring exercises for an infantry regiment in training camp in the late 1930s. Note the coloured 'exercise bands' on the helmets, used to distinguish the opposing sides in mock battles.*

6

mander of the Wehrmacht (armed forces) and established the Oberkommando der Wehrmacht (OKW) as a high command headquarters. The senior generals who queried the wisdom of Hitler's territorial ambitions — on the grounds that the Heer was not yet well enough equipped for full-scale war — were dismissed.

Gen Wilhelm Keitel became the new Chief-of-Staff and Gen Walter von Brauchitsch became C-in-C of the Heer. Both were compliant to Hitler's demands and this set the pattern for Hitler's future command appointments. The international concern arising over Hitler's demands from Czechoslovakia resulted in the Munich agreement of 28 September 1938 whereby Hitler got what he wanted on vague promises of no more aggression. But after taking over the Sudetenland he then moved in and annexed the rest of Czechoslovakia in March 1939, unopposed by any international military moves. In the proce the valuable Czechoslovak arms industry, an much other trade, was acquired for the Great Reich.

Hitler's next target was Poland, with th Danzig Corridor — formerly German territory - as the basis for his demands. It was envisage that Danzig could not be acquired by diplomat means, so a full-scale military campaign to tal Poland was planned. Hitler guessed correctly th Britain and France, Poland's treaty partner would be too weak-willed and lacking in militar strength to aid Poland by attacking from the wes He took care of the Soviet threat from the east b means of furtively planned non-aggression pa with the USSR on 23 August 1939 (the Naz Soviet Pact). This included a secret deal whereb the USSR could occupy the eastern half Poland while Germany took the western half.

THE POLISH CAMPAIGN

An excuse of Polish border intrusion was used to launch a full-scale invasion of Poland on 1 September 1939, with a plan whereby two prongs of advance would encircle and trap most of the lightly equipped Polish army to the west of Warsaw. The military tactics put into practice Guderian's well worked-out theories of fast armoured warfare with air support, and the Blitzkrieg (originally a newspaper description) was born; the word 'Stuka' also passed into the language as the sinister dive-bombers screamed into the attack just in front of the advancing tank columns. In fact, the armoured divisions were relatively restrained in the Polish campaign and were held back so they did not run too far ahead of the infantry divisions and support arms. In Poland this was no great drawback for the Polish Army was relatively poorly equipped and unco-ordinated. It was also having to guard two frontiers, east and west, simultaneously and it proved quite easy for the German forces to split it up and isolate it. On 17 September 1939, the Red Army moved in from the east and secured their segment of the country. On 27 September the last Polish forces surrendered.

The French and British governments, bound by prior treaty to Poland put in an ultimatum to Germany on 1 September 1939, threatening a declaration of war if it was ignored. On 3 September, when the ultimatum expired, it had indeed been ignored by Germany and war was therefore declared by Britain and France against the Third Reich. Hitler had banked on Britain and France taking no action, as had been the case with Czechoslovakia, but even when they did declare war he was confident that his lightning campaign would be over before they could bring material aid to Poland. In this he was correct.

Plate 7: *Invasion of Poland on 1 September 1939: A leutnant of an infantry unit checks his watch for 'zero hour' and the moment to move forward. Note pistol holster on waistbelt and the anti-gas respirator holder and water bottle of the nearer man.*

Plate 8: *Invasion of France in May 1940: artillery of 9th Army crosses the Meuse by pontoon bridge. Note local foliage added to the gun.*

Plate 9: *A 37mm PaK 36 in an ambush position near the French border in the spring of 1940. The nearest man has a band round his helmet to carry camouflage foliage. Note the use of Zeltbahn camouflage shelters in the bushes beyond to form a cubbyhole for the crew.*

Hitler now asked the OKW to plan for an invasion of France, via Belgium, to put his forces into a position from where they could later invade Great Britain. The original notion was to move on to this project immediately after the Polish campaign, but the logistics of moving forces from Poland to the west caused delays, and it was necessary to sit out the winter months and plan for a spring offensive. The October 1939 to April 1940 period was known as the 'Phoney War' as nothing much was happening except for occasional patrol activities. The French Army sat behind the Maginot Line — heavily fortified bunkers along the Franco-German border — while the Germans had the heavily defended Siegfried Line on their side of the border.

The weak point on the Western Front was Belgium, covered largely by the relatively small British Expeditionary Force (BEF) from northern France. As Belgium was officially neutral the BEF could not move into Belgium unless Belgium was also violated. The German invasion plan for France and Flanders bypassed the Maginot Line and would come in through the Ardennes with the main force of Army Group A commanded by Gen Rundstedt. A smaller force, Army Group B, commanded by Gen Bock, would invade Holland to the north.

While planning for this campaign was going on, Hitler also decided to take Denmark and Norway. This was forced upon him by events. The short Russo-Finnish war started on 30 November 1939, following claims by the USSR to Finnish terri-

Plate 10: *German artillery in Norway, late in April 1940, showing equipment slung from waistbelt worn with the greatcoat. Brotbeutel (bread bag), water bottle and gas-mask case are being carried here.*

tory. If Britain and France helped the Finns that might give them access to Germany's northern shores, but more importantly it might deny Germany the vital iron ore supplies that it received from Sweden. Occupying Denmark and Norway (and respecting Sweden's neutrality) was seen as a way of securing the Scandinavian flank and access to the ore supplies.

On 9 April 1940, German forces landed by sea and air in Norway and further south crossed the land border into Denmark. The actual occupation of Denmark was virtually unopposed and concerts by German military bands were a feature of the first day as a means of winning 'hearts and minds'. In Norway, however, there was armed resistance, increased later by the despatch of a hastily organised Anglo-French force to north Norway. Some initial Allied successes, particularly at Narvik, were overcome and the Allies were pulled out after a few weeks of sometimes resourceful, but largely ineffective, effort. The dismal British performance in Norway led to the resignation of the Prime Minister Neville Chamberlain. His notable successor was Winston Churchill who led Britain for the rest of the war period.

THE FRENCH CAMPAIGN

On the day Churchill took office as Prime Minister, 10 May 1940, the German invasion of France and Flanders made a spectacular start. The armoured divisions of Army Group A raced through Belgium and northern France cutting off the British forces (BEF) and some French forces as the tanks broke through to the Channel coast. The fact that Hitler ordered them to stop so that the infantry divisions could catch up saved the BEF by allowing a hastily contrived withdrawal to England via Dunkirk at the end of May 1940.

The German Army Groups now moved south through Sedan and decimated the French divisions by rolling round behind them. Paris was taken on 11 June and the French surrendered on the 22nd. The campaign had barely taken six weeks. The Blitzkrieg tactics tried in Poland but used more extensively in France had paid off, even though they were used more cautiously than they could have been, due to the OKH's constant fear that the armoured divisions would run dangerously ahead of the following infantry divisions which were very dependent on slow moving horse transport.

Plate 11: *Triumph in France; a French Char B tank crew surrender to German troops in June 1940.*

Victory parades were held in Paris and Berlin where Hitler, the Heer and the generals enjoyed acclaim and prestige on a level they would never again achieve. It was the high point of German military success. Hitler now ordered the invasion of Great Britain, codenamed Operation 'Sea Lion', but following the hard-fought Battle of Britain from July to October 1940, this idea was shelved when the Royal Air Force denied the necessary air supremacy to the Luftwaffe.

Plate 12: *Definitely not in the dress regulations is this method of sun protection used by German infantrymen in France, during June 1940, with knotted handkerchiefs on their heads in best British seaside style! Note also the rolled-up jacket sleeves.*

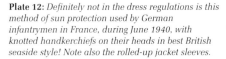

MEDITERRANEAN OPERATIONS

Meanwhile, Italy declared war on Britain and France in June 1940 and Italian forces in Libya threatened British security in Egypt (then a British protectorate). In a bold campaign in December 1940, the British Desert Force (later named the 8th Army) moved into Libya, trounced the Italian Army and almost drove them out. To avoid the embarrassment of an Axis defeat, Hitler sent a German expeditionary force to Libya in January 1941 to help the Italians. This was the famous Afrika Korps, commanded by Gen Erwin Rommel, who had been one of the spearhead Panzer Division commanders (7th Panzer Divi-

sion) in the taking of France. The Afrika Korps, only three divisions strong, but well equipped and superbly led, was quickly able to restore the situation and forced the British back almost to the Egyptian borders.

In April 1941, to secure the Balkans from either British or Soviet occupation, German troops moved into Greece and Jugoslavia, while Luftwaffe airborne forces took the island of Crete. The British forces who had been moved hastily into Greece and Crete were forced to withdraw in some disorder and with heavy loss of equipment.

INVASION OF RUSSIA

Hitler's big objective, however — the non-aggression Nazi-Soviet Pact notwithstanding — was the taking of the USSR. On 22 June 1941 the vast Operation 'Barbarossa' began. To make the best of the 'teeth' arms the Panzer divisions were divided into four groups. The invading armies were organised as three Army Groups, each with an accompanying air fleet. More 'teeth' were given to the infantry divisions in the form of Sturmgeschütz (assault guns) which were either old or captured tank chassis, modified to carry infantry howitzers or tank guns, or purpose-built designs on well proven tank chassis. Hitler committed 145 divisions to battle on the Eastern Front, the greater part of the Heer. About 3 1/4 million men were under arms.

The mighty force moved forward in three thrusts. The objective of Army Group North was to take the Baltic shore and reach Leningrad. For

the biggest formation, Army Group Centre, the objective was to keep north of the Pripet Marshes and head for Smolensk. Army Group South was split into two. One half headed for Kiev and the other half headed southeast.

Like the 1940 invasion of France and Flanders, the opening weeks of Operation 'Barbarossa' were overwhelmingly successful. The Red Army was routed along the entire front and huge numbers of prisoners were taken while big stocks of equipment were siezed. The Red Army, though massive in manpower, was lacking in command and experience because Stalin had carried out a purge of the most experienced officers in 1940 and this deprived the men of good leadership.

Progress was rapid for the German Army. Army Group Centre reached and took Smolensk in just three weeks, but then valuable momentum was lost as Hitler halted it rather than allow it to race on to Moscow while the Soviet High Command was still reeling from the shock of the invasion. This was a costly mistake. Hitler did not order the advance on Moscow to start again until October by which time the Soviets had had time to organise a strong defence, greatly aided, as it turned out, by the hard winter that was fast approaching. This started with heavy rain in October which hampered German progress, followed by a big freeze which started in mid-November.

Though the Red Army had suffered great losses, including whole armies surrounded and taken prisoner, they had great reserves of manpower and some good guns. They were also able to relocate key arms industries well to the east beyond the Urals to replace factories destroyed in the invasion. Above all they had the superb T-34 tank, probably the best tank design of World War 2. It was misused by the Soviets in the opening months of the war, but when improved and built in large numbers in the following years it became the spearhead of the Soviet Army as it steamrollered the German forces back into Germany. The T-34 was superior to any German tank and to combat it the Germans quickly developed the Panther which copied the sloped armour shape of the T-34 but was a much more sophisticated bit of engineering.

The valuable breathing space had allowed the Soviet High Command to muster new forces. In the freezing weather which was discomforting the Germans, they counter-attacked heavily on all fronts during the last week of November. Hitler ordered the generals to stand firm, but Army Group Centre was pushed back 200 miles and suffered heavy losses. One result of this was that Hitler dismissed the C-in-C, Brauchitsch, and most of the senior commanders. He took overall control himself of OKH and Eastern Front operations with Gen Halder as Chief of Staff in the field. The winter campaign was the first major setback for the Wehrmacht since the war began. Losses were very heavy and included over 2,000 AFVs and nearly a million men killed or wounded.

When the good weather returned in May 1942, a new German offensive was launched, but it was carried out by Army Group South where the Soviet opposition was weakest. It was initially very successful, taking many prisoners, occupying the Crimea in June, and moving even further east. The front was now so extended that the Army was divided into two commands, Army Group B to the north and Army Group A in the Caucasus. Stalingrad was considered to be a key objective by Hitler and he ordered the 6th Army, part of Army Group B, to take and hold it. This

Plate 13: *Hitler visits the fighting front: with staff officers and generals he watches reinforcements move up to the frontline in Russia, 1941.*

Plate 14: *The campaign in Russia: assault guns and infantry moving into the heavily damaged outskirts of Stalingrad from which they would not return.*

was achieved after very hard fighting, but the flanks of the lines of communications, vastly overstretched, were also poorly protected, mainly by Romanian and Hungarian volunteer divisions of no great quality. So a determined counter-attack in November 1942 by the Soviet Army had cut through and cut off the 6th Army and its commander, Gen von Paulus, in the Stalingrad pocket. Hitler ordered von Paulus to hold the perimeter and undertook to supply the 6th Army by air. This proved to be an inadequate and hazardous business in the middle of another hard winter. Many aircraft were lost and insufficient supplies got through. A new 'Army Group Don' was established from spare divisions and ordered to fight through to relieve the 6th Army. But this force also failed, halted by the severe winter weather and heavy Soviet pressure. By the year's end, the 6th Army was isolated over 100 miles behind the Soviet frontline.

IN NORTH AFRICA

Things were going badly, too, in North Africa, in 1942. Gen Rommel proved to be a masterly tactician with the Afrika Korps and won great respect, not least from his British opponents, for his resourceful use of a numerically inferior force. After some initial offensives back and forth across Libya, by August 1942 the Afrika Korps stood at Alamein, poised to advance into Egypt. British 8th Army morale was at a low ebb as the next German offensive was awaited. However, fortunes changed: a dynamic new commander, Gen Bernard Montgomery, was appointed to command the 8th Army and this coincided with the availability of much-needed new equipment, notably the Sherman tank and huge numbers of guns. Hitler had declared war on the United States of America in December 1941 and this was the most costly of all his mistakes. He assumed that America would have to concentrate all its military effort in the Pacific war against Japan, but he underestimated American resources.

Plate 15: *A VW Kubelwagen on patrol at the height of the desert war in 1942, with the men all wearing the lightweight tropical uniform with long trousers. Their helmets seem to be still in field grey finish as is the interior of the vehicle and the jerrican.*

21

Through 1942 there was a big build-up of US forces in Britain ready for a 'second front' in Europe. Vast amounts of armaments became available to British and Commonwealth forces under Lend-Lease arrangements from America 'the arsenal of democracy' as the American President Roosevelt described it.

With the big build-up of aid, the 8th Army launched a colossal offensive in late October 1942 and finally rolled the much-pounded Afrika Korps back across Libya. In early November Anglo-American forces landed in Morocco and Algeria in Operation 'Torch' and pushed the German forces from the opposite direction. In January 1943 the remnants of the Afrika Korps had to evacuate to Italy and Germany had been defeated — with big losses of men and equipment — in North Africa.

Plate 16: *Afrika Korps generals surrender to the British in Tunisia, early in 1943. They are wearing the lightweight tropical uniform and the later cheaper version of the greatcoat without facing material. Note the piping on the centre general's Feldmütze. In the background is a captured colonel.*

SETBACKS IN RUSSIA

Worse was to come on the Russian Front. The 6th Army, besieged in Stalingrad in a nightmare of cold, starvation and heavy pounding was unable to hold out any longer and von Paulus surrendered at the end of January 1943. It was a major triumph for the Soviet Union and a massive humiliation for Hitler, Germany and the Heer. Of 280,000 men in the 6th Army only 91,000 remained to surrender and of these only 5,000 survived the privations of Russian prison camps to return to Germany years later.

In an attempt to restore German military fortunes, Hitler gave the tank expert Guderian the post of Inspector General of Panzer Troops to co-ordinate and control all Panzer divisions. He also ordered the expansion of the Waffen-SS to form more armoured divisions and gave it priority of equipment. Goering, the Luftwaffe commander, was also instrumental in an expansion of Luftwaffe ground forces to provide a Panzer division and, eventually, 19 Luftwaffe infantry divisions. While all this put more troops on the ground, it also dissipated lines of command and control.

For the 1943 Eastern Front offensive it was decided to eliminate the Kursk salient, the area resolutely held by the Soviets since the previous summer's offensive. Called Operation 'Citadel', the plan was to envelop Kursk in a pincer movement using the 9th Army from the north and the 4th Army from the south. However, the start was

Plate 17: *The severe winter weather in Russia led to the development of the two-piece winter suit for the second winter, 1942-43. This was white on one side and grey or camouflaged on the other. Note the coloured identification strips buttoned onto the sleeves.*

Plate 18: *The poor quality of the 1943 service dress is apparent on these prisoners captured in Russia in February 1944. Only the centre man in the front row wears the 1935 pattern service dress, all the others being in the inferior 1943 version. Note third man from left, front row, wearing the green mosquito net as a head covering.*

elayed until 4 July to enable new heavy tanks d assault guns (Tiger tanks, Elefant SPs) to be ployed. By the time Operation 'Citadel' had

late 19: *The fighting in Russia was dominated by ud and bad weather. Here a Tiger tank and infantry ove through a village in late 1943. The nearest man rries a box of MG34 ammunition slung from a ovel. The man on the extreme right has the folded MG34 tripod on his back.*

begun the Soviets had themselves built up superior forces for an offensive they were planning. They gained air superiority and heavy rain disrupted the German attack and bogged down vehicles. Soviet counter-attacks were carried out and on 25 July the Germans were forced to withdraw after very heavy losses including over 1,000 tanks and nearly half-a-million men dead or wounded.

By this time Germany was being harried on a new front. Allied troops landed in Sicily in July

1943 and on 3 September they landed in Italy on the day the Italians had arranged to surrender to the Allies. Foreseeing this possibility Hitler had moved more German divisions into Italy, so at the time of the Italian surrender they were well deployed to resist. The Allies had a very tough job fighting the German forces in an advance north through Italy, mostly over unfriendly terrain. It took until nearly the end of the war in Europe. German forces, too, were involved in holding Jugoslavia and the rest of the Balkans against increasing opposition, mostly from Tito's resistance fighters in the case of Jugoslavia.

These new fronts diverted forces away from the Eastern Front and made that theatre increasingly untenable. Following the success at K[ursk] and with an increasing build-up of forces equipment, the Soviets now began to push depleted German forces out of Russia. Hitler insistence that generals stand their ground not help for it denied the field commanders chance to shorten their lines of communication or find better defence lines if they saw fit May 1944 most German forces in Russia were steady retreat, but those in the Crimea were encircled and captured.

INVASION OF EUROPE

In June 1944 came the move which signalled the impending end of the Third Reich. On 6 June 1944, Allied forces landed in Normandy in the great Operation 'Overlord' invasion. Well organised and commanded in the field by Montgomery, the victor of Alamein, the Allies were quickly established on the beach-head to begin the push eastwards into Germany. The western coast of Europe, rather grandly called the 'Atlantic Wall' by the Germans, had been fortified against invasion since 1940. In 1944 the area commander was Rommel, the former Afrika Korps commander.

Keeping the Germans guessing was part of the plan and among other feints was the build-up of

non-existent forces (indicated by fake signal fic) in East Anglia to create an impression the invasion would take place in the Calais a In addition, Hitler had the idea that the invas would come through Norway, so he placed forces there. Once the Allies were ashore the C mans now had the tough problems of conduc a war on two fronts, doomed to being crus

Plate 20: *An Army AA gun mounted on a half-track France in 1944. The men are wearing the 1943 pattern uniform with ankle boots and gaiters. A camouflage pattern is daubed on the helmets to match the vehicle pattern.*

ween forces pushing from both west and east.
he west there were weaknesses as many divi-
1s were below strength, having been 'milked'
men to send to the Russian Front. There were,
vever, well equipped Panzer divisions with
er and Panther tanks.

Not knowing from where the invasion would
1e was a problem, of course, with conflict-
opinions leading to confused command
isions. Rommel, the field commander for
Channel coast, wanted to fight on the
ches to deny the invaders a foothold. His
mander, Rundstedt, the C-in-C West,
ated to deploy his strength inland to draw
invaders into a trap. Hitler imposed his
ws above everybody else and drew the
zer divisions well back so that they could
ve in any necessary direction. Valuable time
lost, too, when Hitler and others thought
Normandy landings were a diversion for a
landing nearer Calais. However, Normandy
ved to be the real thing and the fighting
intense. In the circumstances the record of
Heer was honourable and brave. Outnum-
ed, the troops fought well and Caen, a piv-

otal point, held out for months against constant
heavy pounding.

The 3rd US Army, under the dynamic Gen
George Patton, eventually broke out of the Normandy bridgehead at St Lô and rolled up behind
the Germans. The only escape for the trapped
German divisions was through the Falaise Gap
where they were bombed and systematically
picked off. Over 50,000 men were captured and
much equipment was destroyed. The Allies had
complete air superiority and lack of fuel and aircraft meant that the Luftwaffe could only offer
token activity. The Cherbourg peninsula was cut
off and the German forces there were captured.
Later the same thing happened at the more
northerly Channel ports. The Allies took the
whole of France, bringing in further invasion
forces on the Mediterranean coast to secure the
south. There was no success for the German
forces until September/October 1944 when the
overstretched Allies attempted to secure a Rhine
bridgehead by taking the Dutch bridges by
parachute assault. At Arnhem they were held up
by German troops reacting decisively and the
Allied momentum was halted.

RUSSIAN OFFENSIVE

the east the Soviets continued their great
nsive. In late June 1944 a big assault on Army
up Centre virtually destroyed it as a fighting
e. A further offensive in July pushed the Ger-
n forces back into Poland and Czechoslovakia.
August the Russians were approaching War-
y, but they made no attempt to help the Polish
derground Army which rose up against the
mans, confident of Russian help. Cynically
Russians held back and the revolt was bru-
y put down by Waffen-SS divisions.
'urther south the Romanian Army, which had
ght the war allied to Germany, changed sides

and joined the Russians. This trapped the German troops in Romania and led to further large
losses.

With the situation worsening by the week and
the fighting getting perilously close to German
soil, Hitler announced the formation of the
Volkssturm in October 1944. This was a German
version of the Home Guard, manned by all men
in the 16-60 age range not already called up. To
make up numbers, too, all sorts of 'ersatz' units
had been formed, including even boys of 16 or
under in the Hitler Youth.

BATTLE OF THE BULGE

pace of Allied advance on the Western Front
slowed down with the approach of winter
Hitler took one last gamble to win back the
. He called up all available reserves for a bold
nsive against the American front in the
ennes on 16 December 1944 — the so-called
le of the Bulge — whereby he hoped to drive
edge between the US 1st Army and the British
Army to the north of them, the object being
reach the coast at Antwerp and divide the
es completely. Because bad weather stopped
ed air operations, the bold move almost suc-
ded but once Allied aircraft could operate
in the Germans were driven back with over

100,000 casualties. Though they had given the
Americans a severe blow, with 75,000 casualties,
the German losses could be ill-afforded when
they lost around 800 tanks as well. These numbers could never be made good at this late stage
of the war.

By the end of 1944 there had been over two
million casualties of all sorts on both Eastern and
Western Fronts in the six months since the Allied
invasion. The Heer was now reduced to a piece-
meal collection of variously equipped units, all
much under strength. Morale was at a low ebb as
depleted ammunition and fuel stocks restricted
operations still further.

25

The new year, 1945, saw another mighty Russian offensive open up, with advances into Silesia, East Prussia and Hungary. Early in February 1945 the Soviets crossed the River Oder and were poised for the final push to Berlin. Meanwhile the Allied forces in the west crossed the Rhine and were also pushing across Germany towards Berlin. Early in April 1945, the British encircled and captured the entire Army Group B (of 300,000 men) in the Ruhr. A week later the Red Army had Berlin surrounded and besieged while other divisions swept on round it heading west to join up with the British and US Armies. The first contact was made on 25 April 1945 and the Allies ended up dividing the parts of Germany they had captured on a line roughly north-south of the rivers Elbe and Mulde.

Sheltering in his command bunker in Berlin with the city shattered around him and the Volkssturm and assorted Heer units fighting against overwhelming odds, Hitler committed suicide on 30 April 1945, appointing Admiral Doenitz, the navy commander, as his successor. On the previous day the German forces in Northern Italy had surrendered and there was now virtually nothing left to fight for. Only a few isolated pockets of German resistance remained. On 7 May 1945, Doenitz signed an act of unconditional surrender with the British and American allies and all hostilities ended the following day, 8 May. A day later the surrender was also signed with the Russians in Berlin who had captured the city on 2 May. The war in Europe was over,

as was the tenure of the Third Reich and, f time being, the German Army had ceased to as a fighting force.

Though finally defeated by the enormous stacked against it, the Heer acquitted itself The German soldier proved to be a dough determined fighter right to the end. These ties made him a tough opponent both in v and defeat. This was largely due to cha building and thorough military training than a fanaticism for the Nazi cause, even th Hitler did provide charismatic leadership ir lier days which appealed to many. In tra and in service, the Germans emphasised spirit in small self-contained units — the E principle — which gave a good sense of pu and comradeship to the individual soldier Heer was also skilfully promoted to the p both in peace and war, and this did muc morale. Individual responsibility was p right down to the lower ranks, and the prop of staff officers and HQ staffs was lower i Heer than in most other armies. The clas tinction between officers and men, too, much less marked in the German Army th others. All personnel could be awarded the medals and all junior officers had served in in the ranks. Much was done to emphasis old traditions in the Army of the Third I When the old Imperial national colours revived so were the honours and traditions old Imperial regiments, and these were pass to the new regiments of the Heer. Modern of dignity were written into the military There were no degrading field punishments old, nor were there any military detention tres. Dishonourable conduct led to dism though in the war years there were some pu ment battalions formed and bad behaviour result in reduction in rank. The idea was lished that to belong to the Heer was an h and the smartness and quality of the unifor much to emphasise this.

Plate 21: *A divisional commander confers with s of his regimental officers from his staff car. The general is on the footboard of the car at right an of his staff officers, wearing an aiguilette, is in th back of the car. His driver is on the right. Note th divisional commander's pennant and tactical sig (right) and Heer pennant marking (WH — Wehr Heer) on the left.*

2. Command and Organisation

Adolf Hitler, the Führer, was considerably ahead of contemporary military thought in 1935 when he expanded and reorganised the armed forces of the Third Reich as a unified command. He was, however, in a better position than most military leaders to do so. In creating a 'new' air force (Luftwaffe) and navy (Kriegsmarine) and greatly expanding the existing army he was starting virtually afresh with no established command staffs having vested positions to maintain who could delay or obstruct the new plans. In the new 1935 organisation the armed forces (Die Wehrmacht) were under unified command and the army (Das Heer) were a part of it. Hitler, as Führer, was also the Supreme Commander of all armed forces, thus combining political and military will as one. Members of the armed forces no longer took an oath of allegiance to the State but to the Führer, Hitler, personally, he being considered the supreme arbiter of national policy and objectives.

OKW

The overall command was vested in the High Command of the Armed Forces (Oberkommando der Wehrmacht - OKW) who was responsible for the complete organisation, co-ordination and deployment of the armed forces. For a key part of the war during 1942-43, Generalfeldmarschal Wilhelm Keitel was C-in-C of the Wehrmacht answering directly to Hitler, and to a great exten subservient to Hitler's will.

SERVICE COMMANDS

Answering to the OKW were the High Commands of the three branches of armed forces, Heer, Luftwaffe and Kriegsmarine. Thus there was an Army High Command (Oberkommando des Heeres) with its own general staff and C-in-C who carried out control of the army to meet the directives set out by the High Command of the Armed Forces (OKW). There were similar command structures for the Luftwaffe and Kriegsmarine and the accompanying table shows the chain of command, with the names of the respective C-in-C and chiefs of staff at roughly the mid-point of World War 2, summer 1943.

It will be noted that Hitler appears as C-in-C of the Army at this time and this indicates what many in the German armed forces at the time thought a weakness of the system. With unchallenged supreme power, Hitler could interfere an take charge at will, firing generals at a whim for single poor performance on the battlefield an rarely taking into account the circumstances c failure. He also got rid of those who did not shar his optimism or counselled caution when Hitle himself took a more simplistic view of the pote tial for success. Hence there were quite frequer changes of command at OKH and Army leve Generals who went along with Hitler's optimist view generally got command or senior staff pos and lasted until the next battlefield setback whe somebody else replaced them. In 1943 Hitle replaced the head of OKH, Halder, and too direct command himself. Gen Zeitzler, a fair junior general who agreed with Hitler was give accelerated promotion and made Chief of Staff

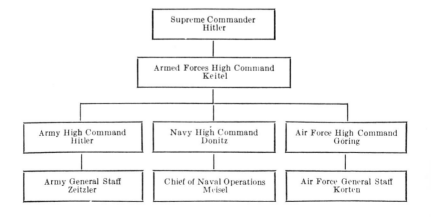

KH and, in effect, became Hitler's 'voice' at ▪adquarters since Hitler did not take up a full-ne post at OKH due to his many other activi-▪s.

The result of the changes of command and ▪tler's ability to switch between OKW and OKH, ▪metimes playing off one against the other, was ▪cause frequent confusion and indecision. ▪dded to this was further complication when ▪ftwaffe field divisions served with the Heer, ▪rected by Oberkommando der Luftwaffe (OKL) ▪t under local Army command. Waffen-SS divi-▪ns were similarly, and even more wilfully, ▪posed to further confuse command divisions. ▪erefore the flexibility and clear lines of com-▪and which the unified command system

promised were not so clear-cut in practice as they were on paper.

In addition Hitler most often exercised his executive power in the field through his Field Headquarters (Feldhauptquartier) which included OKW staff officers, staff officers of all three forces, personal staff officers, political officials and others. This headquarters was something of a moving 'circus' which went wherever Hitler went, and he was often restless. The chain of command was sometimes disrupted further by Hitler's interference in trivial detail while key decisions went unanswered, or yesterday's decisions were reversed if Hitler consulted a more forceful staff officer with more attractive ideas than the previous one!

CHAIN OF COMMAND

theory the chain of command and decision as ▪d down by Hitler and his staff took the follow-▪g operational procedure:

▪. Hitler's military objective was put to the head of OKW;

▪. The head of OKW called for a staff appreciation of the problem and specified the objective;

▪. The three service High Commands (OKH, OKL, OKW) were called in to discuss inter-service needs and potential of the problem (for example a bombing campaign needed, or a port to be bombarded);

▪. If Hitler accepted the staff appreciation and outline plan he would appoint a commander for the operation depending on service emphasis;

▪. The commander was appointed and given the objective. He then answered directly to OKW, whatever his previous status.;

▪. The operational commander established a staff to draw up detailed plans and requirements;

▪. The operational plans were submitted to OKW (and therefore, usually to Hitler, too) for final approval;

▪. Specific units required were called in, positioned, trained, deployed and designated for the role — for example Army Group B;

9. Hitler and the OKW gave final approval and set dates and timetables based on the detailed planning;

10. This was 'D-Day' for the operation.

This procedure was nominally followed whether the matter concerned was a complete campaign or a local offensive by one Army or Army Group. In practice indecision or changes of mind, particularly in the latter half of the war quite often disrupted planning or the timetables as at Operation 'Citadel', the Battle of Kursk in July 1943, when valuable impetus was lost (as was the battle) due to a last-minute decision to hold back so that new heavy tanks and assault guns could be delivered.

Also, in the latter half of the war the massive attrition, particularly on the Eastern Front, and fast-moving action often prevented proper planning. Many engagements and attacks were of an ad hoc nature, hastily cobbled up and conducted by any available units in the theatre of war. In the last couple of years of the war, many army divisions were well below strength (sometimes as few as 1,000 men in what was nominally a division) and the theoretical approach was frequently ignored.

OKH

▪e Oberkommando des Heeres (OKH) was the ▪dividual High Command for the Army, sub-▪rvient to OKW but otherwise entirely responsi-▪e for all aspects of army command, administra-▪n, organisation, and training. The C-in-C of the ▪my headed OKH. There were eight sections:
Adjutant's Office (Adjtantur) — this was a

clearing department for all mail and communications concerning OKH
2. Personnel Office (Personalamt) — this was the department dealing with all officers' appointments and reports up to the rank of Oberstleutnant (Lt-Col). It was also responsible for promotions, transfers and retirements, etc. An

exception was officers (of any rank) in the General Staff Corps who were appointed and commended for promotion personally by the Chief of General Staff, and colonels and generals who were personally appointed or approved by Hitler

3. General Staff (Generalstab) — the Chief of Staff was responsible for five administrative departments, each under control of a Deputy Quartermaster General (Oberquartermeister). Each department was further subdivided into sections (Abteilungen) in the following order:

Oberquartiermeister I — Operations
Abteilung 1 — Operations
Abteilung 5 — Transport
Abteilung 6 — Rear Echelons
Abteilung 9 — Topography
Abteilung 10 — Exercises and Operational Planning

Oberquartiermeister II — Training
Abteilung 4 — Training
Abteilung 11 — Military Schools and Officers' Training

Oberquartiermeister III — Organisation
Abteilung 2 — Organization
Abteilung 8 — Technical Services

Oberquartiermeister IV — Intelligence
Abteilung 3 — Eastern Section
Abteilung 12 — Western Section

Oberquartiermeister V — Historical
Abteilung 7 — Historical

4. The General Army Office (Allgemeines Heersamt) — this was the department charged with maintaining standards and allocating defence funding. The various Inspector Generals and their staffs came within this department. The following sections were under command of the Allgemeines Heersamt:

I — Central Section, including Army Publications Administration
II — Budget Section of the Army
III — Mobilisation and Organisation Section
IV — Ordnance Inspectorate
V — Inspectorate of Infantry
VI — Inspectorate of Cavalry and Horse-drawn Transport
VII — Inspectorate of Artillery
VIII — Inspectorate of Engineers
IX — Inspectorate of Fortresses
X — Weapons Section of the Panzer Troops, Cavalry, and Army Motorisation

XI — Inspectorate of Signal Troops
XII — Inspectorate of Transport Troops
XIII — Inspectorate of Chemical Warfare Troops
XIV — Inspectorate of Railway Engineers
XV — Medical Inspectorate
XVI — Veterinary Inspectorate

5. Ordnance Office (Waffenamt) — this divisi[] of the OKH was responsible for developme[] testing, research, regulations, etc, with the f[] lowing eight sections under command:

I — Raw Materials Section
II — Chief Engineer's Office
III — Periodicals Section
IV — Regulations Section
V — Research Section
VI — Development and Testing Group (with 12 sub-sections which deal wi[] the weapons for various arms)
VII — Industrial Mobilisation Group
VIII — Acceptance Section

6. Administration Office (Heeres-Verw[] tungsamt) — property, civilian employees and food and supply acquisition was the responsib[] ity of this department with the following fo[] sections:

I — Army Civilian Officials, Employees, and Finance
II — Food and Supplies
III — Barracks and Training Grounds
IV — Administration of Army Buildings

7. Chief of the Mobile Troops (Chef d[] Schnellen Truppen) — this was a later depa[] ment set up in 1938 to administer the gr[] expansion of panzer divisions and other mech[] nised troops which were forming the spearhe[] of the army. It was responsible for training a[] development of panzer troops, cavalry (a[] mechanised cavalry), motor reconnaissance a[] armoured car troops, and motor-cycle troops.

In 1943, in recognition of the ever increasi[] importance of the panzer divisions, this depa[] ment was largely supplemented in its functio[] by the newly created Inspector General Armoured Forces (General Inspekteur für c Panzerwaffe) with wide powers of command a[] answering directly to Hitler whose idea it w[] The first holder of this appointment was G[] Heinz Guderian, the army's foremost expert armoured warfare

8. Inspectorate of Cadet Schools (Inspektion d[] Kriegschulen) — as is self-evident from its tit[] this department was responsible for junior a[] entry officer training

---

SUBORDINATE COMMANDS

Armies and Army Corps had a Chief of Staff in charge of all staff and staff matters. Divisions did not have a designated Chief of Staff. His duties were carried out by the senior General St[] Corps officer who had the appointment of Seni[] Staff officer (Operations), a term often encou[]

tered in reports of events, and very often shortened to just 'la'.

All Army, Army Corps and Divisional staffs were organised in a similar way as follows.

1. Section I General Staff (Generalstab) — composed of General Staff Corps officers it was divided into four sections:

    1a — Operations (senior staff officer)
    1b — Supply and Administration
    1c — Intelligence
    1d — Training

A reference in a report to, say, '1c' would be a shorthand way of indicating the Intelligence Officer. The General Staff section did not get involved in routine matters. The 'la' was always considered the senior post. In Army Corps and Armies the la was the deputy to the Chief of Staff and acted in his absence. In a Division the la was, in effect, the Chief of Staff though not known as such

2. Section II Adjutant's Office (Adjutantur) — this was section concerned with routine administration and was headed by a qualified General Staff Corps officer

3. Section III Legal Section (Feldjustizamt) — this was the legal branch, staffed mainly by civilian officials (Beamten) in uniform

4. Section IV Intendants (Intendantur) — this section administered the key supply, medical and veterinary services and was staffed by specialist officers in these fields

5. Section V Religious Services (Wehrmachtsseelorgedienst) — this was staffed by Army chaplains of various denominations depending on religious composition of the command.

There were three staff sub-divisions for specific functions:

1. Tactical Group (Führungs-Abteilung) — this was made up of la and 1c staff Section I

2. Supply Group (Quartiermeister-Abteilung) — this was made up of lb of staff Section I and all of staff Section IV

3. Personnel Group (Adjutantur) — this was made up of the whole of staff Sections II, III and V. In addition the postal section, pay section, divisional services and divisional HQ troops were attached to this Group.

ATTACHED STAFF OFFICERS

Depending on the formation there were officers attached to various staffs as follows:

1. Army — senior officers respectively from cavalry (if appropriate), armour, artillery, anti-tank, engineers and signal troops. These officers were appointed as technical advisers to the Army Commander in all matters related to their specialist arms. They were known as the Höherer Artilleriekommandeur (Senior Artillery Commander), etc

2. Army Corps — to each Corps HQ was appointed a senior officer of engineers, anti-tank and signal troops. They answered to the Chief of Staff of the Corps, but they also commanded the Corps units of their respective arms. They advised both the Corps Commander and Divisional Commanders within the Corps. The appointment was known as Kommandeur der

Pioneere (Commander of Engineers), etc

3. Division — at divisional level a senior artillery officer was appointed as Artillerie-Führer (Artillery Leader) who was both the commander of divisional artillery and the artillery adviser to the Divisional Commander. In addition there was a Divisional Artillery Officer, Divisional Engineer Officer, Divisional Signal Officer, Divisional Transport Officer and Divisional Anti-Tank Officer who were usually the senior officers of their specialisation within the division who were attached to the Tactical Group of the divisional staff as required. Further to this the Commander of the Divisional Train, the Divisional Provost Marshal, the Divisional Postal Commander and a senior engineer officer and a senior signal officer were attached to the Supply Group of the divisional staff as required.

DISTRICTS

Within Germany itself the country was divided into military districts (Wehrkreise) which was related both to the garrison organisation and recruiting areas. In peacetime each Wehrkreise had an appointed commander who also in time of war became the Corps Commander on mobilisation for the Corps having the same number as the Wehrkreise. The deputy commander of the Wehrkreise took over command of the

Wehrkreise on mobilisation in place of the original Wehrkreise commander. He then became responsible for recruiting and training within the Wehrkreise, for maintaining the supply of new troops required as replacements, and for military expansion. The army in the field was known as the Feldheer (Field Army), and the reserves and recruits, being recruited and trained within each Wehrkreise, were collectively known as the

Ersatzheer (Replacement Army). The General Army Office in Berlin (Allgemeines Heersamt) co-ordinated recruiting and training policy. The Wehrkreise (Military Districts) on the outbreak of war in September 1939 are shown in the table below:

Wehrkreis	Area included	Headquarters of Wehrkreis and of Corps	Peacetime garrison divisions
I	East Prussia	Königsberg	1st, 11th and 21st, and 1st Cavalry Brigade
II	Pomerania and Mecklenburg	Stettin	2nd, 12th and 32nd
III	Brandenburg	Berlin	3rd and 23rd and 3rd Panzer and 3rd Light
IV	Saxony and North Sudetenland	Dresden	4th, 14th and 24th
V	Southwest Germany	Stuttgart	5th, 25th and 35th
VI	Westphalia and Lower Rhineland	Münster	6th, 16th and 26th and 1st Light
VII	Upper Bavaria	München (Munich)	7th and 27th, and 1st Mountain
VIII	Silesia and East Sudetenland	Breslau	8th, 18th and 28th, and 5th Panzer
IX	Hesse and Thuringia	Kassel	9th, 15th and 29th, and 2nd Light and 1st Panzer
X	Schleswig-Holstein and North Sea coastal area	Hamburg	10th, 20th and 22nd
XI	Hannover and Prussian Saxony	Hannover	13th, 19th and 31st
XII	Middle Rhineland	Wiesbaden	33rd, 34th and 36th
XIII	Franconia and West Sudetenland	Nürnberg (Nuremburg)	10th, 17th and 46th and 4th Panzer
XVII	Upper and Lower Austria	Wien (Vienna)	44th and 45th and 2nd Panzer and 4th Light
XVIII	Tyrol, Carinthia and Styria	Salzburg	2nd and 3rd Mountain

Following the war conquests there were some additional military districts designated in the newly acquired areas. Wehrkreis XX covered Danzig, Wehrkreis XXI covered Posen, Alsace was incorporated into Wehrkreis V, Lorraine and Luxembourg were incorporated into Wehrkreis XII, Eupen-Malmedy was incorporated into Wehrkreis VI, part of North Jugoslavia into Wehrkreis XVIII, and the Bialystok area into Wehrkreis I.

The four 'missing' numbers in the Wehrkreis series were Corps numbers only, though headquartered in specific cities, but they were reserved to cover command of the prewar tank, light and motorised divisions, as below:

Corps	Corps headquarters	Divisions supervised
XIV	Magdeburg	2nd, 13th, 20th and 29th Motorised
XV	Jena	1st, 2nd, 3rd and 4th Light
XVI	Berlin	1st, 2nd, 3rd, 4th and 5th Panzer
XIX	Wien (Vienna)	New formations

RECRUITMENT

From 1919 to 1935 service with the Reichsheer was voluntary only. Under the new Third Reich regime the new military law introduced on 21 May 1935 made military service compulsory, if required, for all men in the 18-45 age band. German men reaching 18 had to register officially (the Musterung). Conscription originally was for one year but from 1936 this became two years. After medical examination men passed fit could be called up (Einberufung) in peacetime at the age of 20. Pending that any man who did not have civilian work would be drafted into the National Labour Service (Reichsarbeitsdienste) to await actual induction to the army on reaching 20. When the war started this procedure was modified and men went straight into the army or registering at 18. Also, during the war years, the upper age limit could be extended by government decree. Keen volunteers in the war years could also enlist at 17. In early 1943 the upper age limit for men joining fighting arms was reduced to 37, or 33 in tropical areas.

All men aged 18 or over were placed in a military category which was shown with their particulars in official documents and registers. Only invalids were exempt from classification. The official categories were as follows:

Aktiv Dienende — on active service
Reserve I — fully trained, under 35
Reserve II — partially trained under 35
Ersatzreserve I — untrained, not called up, under 35
Ersatzreserve II — untrained, physically unfit, under 35
Landwehr I — trained, between 35 and 45
Landwehr II — untrained between 35 and 45
Landsturm I — trained, over 45
Landsturm II — untrained, over 45

During the war years all the men on the list down to the category of Landwehr II were likely to be called to active service.

Every Wehrkreise was sub-divided into recruiting areas (Wehrersatzbezirke) and these were further divided into sub-areas (Wehrbezirke). The recruiting areas were as follows:

Wehrkreis	Wehrersatzbezirk	Number of Wehrbezirke
I	Königsberg	7
I	Allenstein	4
II	Stettin	12
II	Schwerin	4
III	Berlin	10
III	Frankfurt-am-Oder	5
III	Potsdam	7
IV	Leipzig	11
IV	Dresden	12
IV	Chemnitz	9
V	Ulm	10
V	Stuttgart	13
VI	Münster	11
VI	Dortmund	8
VI	Düsseldorf	14
VI	Köln (Cologne)	9
VII	München (Munich)	12
VIII	Breslau	13
VIII	Kattowitz	13
VIII	Liegnitz	7
IX	Kassel	9
IX	Frankfurt-am-Main	6
IX	Weimar	9
X	Schleswig-Holstein	6
X	Hamburg	6
X	Bremen	9
XI	Hannover	8
XI	Magdeburg	7
XII	Koblenz	10
XII	Mannheim	10
XIII	Regensburg	5
XIII	Nürnburg (Nuremburg)	11
XIII	Karlsbad	5
XVII	Linz	5
XVII	Wien (Vienna)	12
XVIII	Innsbruck	3
XVIII	Graz	10
XX	Danzig	7
XXI	Posen	5

As with the Wehrkreise allocations, numbers XIV, XV, XVI and XIX are missing from the list. They were the Corps covering armour, light and motorised units which recruited from all over Germany and not from any designated area.

OFFICERS

In peacetime, officer candidates for the 'teeth' arms were commissioned after being selected as officer candidates and serving four years in the ranks with exemplary service. In wartime, officer candidates were commissioned from the ranks after one tour of service at the front followed by a five-month officer training course. Specialist officers (medical, chaplain, etc) were normally commissioned directly after obtaining their qualifications as a civilian.

In addition there were many categories of specialisation (eg lawyers, architects, land conservators etc) who were appointed for their particular skills but were categorised as 'Army Officials' (Beamten) and enjoyed officer status in most cases, though some lower grades were rated as NCO equivalents. Another category, particularly prevalent in the wartime years, was the Sonderführer (Special Leader) who wore officer-style uniforms and enjoyed officer status without being actually commissioned as an officer. The officer status was, however, considered desirable for the importance of their duties. Typical Sonderführer posts were army war reporters or photographers, temporarily employed dentists and medical specialists and so on. Further details are given in the descriptions of uniforms and insignia later in the book.

33

NCOS

NCOs in peacetime were selected from volunteers only who joined the Heer for a 12-year engagement. Selected senior NCOs could have their engagement extended to 25 years. During the war years NCOs could be promoted from any suitable candidate and they were given a nominal 4½-year 'regular' engagement. Any man could apply to become a NCO. After satisfactory 'acting'

service as a Gefreiter he could be promoted to Unteroffizier if recommended by his company commander. In peacetime there were also NCO schools taking candidates from the ranks between the ages of 18 and 20. They were given a two-year course and promoted Unteroffizier on satisfactory completion. In wartime the courses were shortened considerably.

TRAINING

In the Third Reich era, prior to the outbreak of war, nearly all Heer recruits had preliminary service in the National Labour Service so they already had some experience of military discipline and organisation. Recruits in peacetime had a five-month initial training. The last month involved full field training.

In the period 1 April to 1 August, in peacetime, every active Heer regiment was sent to training camp for three weeks under canvas during which period inter-arms training usually took place. Each camp area held three regiments so for the three-week period the camp might be shared by, say, an infantry regiment, a cavalry regiment and an artillery battalion, and they would exercise together in simulated combat. Divisional manoeuvres took place in September and October. Army manoeuvres were held in alternate years and Corps manoeuvres were held in two or three Werkreise each year.

DIVISIONAL ORGANISATION

In both peace and war German divisional organisation was changing all the time in greater or smaller measure. This flexibility was deliberate to take best advantage of new developments and changing tactical requirements. Some changes were forced by events, most notably in the final year of the war when manpower was short, casualties were high, and for the most part German forces were fighting a losing battle. A characteristic fighting unit of the era was the Kampfgruppe (Battle Group) which had no definite organic establishment and was an ad hoc formation made up of whatever units might be to hand to throw into action. In that period, too, even organic divisions were usually well below strength and some elements of the division could be either nominal or missing completely.

In normal conditions, however, the composition of German fighting units was based on the Einheit (unit) principle. The theory of this was that standard types of small unit with standard organisation, training and equipment were adopted as a basis on which all larger formations were built. The basic infantry unit was the platoon, comprising four rifle sections each with a light machine gun (MG34 or MG42) team, plus a light mortar section. This basic unit was the foundation of all other arms in which tactical employment was based on firepower and movement. Thus this basic unit was found in the infantry, motorised infantry, motor-cycle companies, engineer companies and all signal units.

The same principle was applied to field and combat trains. The train (Tross) of each company, troop or battery was organised identically, the only difference being in the mode of transport (eg, horse, lorry, half-track). Each train was composed of three Einheit groups. These were the Gefechts-Tross (combat train), Verpflegungs-Tross (ration train) and Gepäck-Tross (baggage train). All battalion, regimental or divisional ammunition or service trains were based on the standard light column which was a complete operating unit of 15, 30 or 60 tons load capacity. All supplies were made up for issue and carriage in 30-ton lots. The advantage of this Einheit principle was that training and tactical employment could be standardised throughout the Heer and in all branches. Flexibility was achieved by the ability to form larger units by combining the standard units as required.

Each combat unit from the basic infantry platoon to a complete division was organised, armed and equipped so that it could operate independently, carrying all necessary weapons and ammunition to carry out its task.

Similarly, in the case of personnel and transport, each tactical unit responsible for administration was so organised as to be independent of the next higher unit. The administrative units were the Army, the Division and the Battalion. All other tactical units were attached to one of these three formations for administration or supply. Each of these administrative units had to

Plate 22: *A divisional command post. This is the SdKfz 251/6 half-track of a panzer division commander, displaying the appropriate metal command pennant, pictured during Rommel's offensive of January-February 1942. The general (in tropical helmet) is partly hidden leaning against the half-track, conferring with staff officers.*

draw its supplies from the next higher administrative unit, and each was equipped with sufficient transport for this task. This principle, together with formation of the divisional trains into as many light columns as there were battalions in a division, made German tactical units very flexible.

With the administrative independence of the battalion, a widely varying number of battalions could be grouped under a single regimental headquarters (British equivalent, Brigade HQ) with their proportionate share of light columns attached to the divisional trains without placing any further strain on the system. This principle made the reinforcement of artillery firepower very easy and allowed any division to be expanded or reduced very quickly to suit current tactical needs.

Each division could also be broken down easily into two or more self-sufficient battle groups. In the case of an infantry division this comprised the infantry regiment reinforced by a battalion of light field howitzers and the option of an attached anti-tank gun company, and an engineer company.

The types of division most commonly found in the Heer were: Infantry, Motorised, Panzer (armoured), Mountain, Light, Cavalry and Reserve. Of these the last cavalry division, 1 Kavallerie-Division, was converted to tanks in 1942 as the 24th Panzer-Division

---

CORPS AND ARMIES

The Division was the basic large formation of the Heer. Two or more Divisions could be grouped together to form a Corps. Each Corps command normally had a signal battalion and various service units attached.

Two or more Corps could be grouped together to form an Army. Each Army command had a signal regiment and various administrative units attached. Specific to Germany was the designation Panzer Army (Panzer Armee) in the case of Corps groups with a large proportion of Panzer Divisions under command.

Two or more Armies could be placed together to form an Army Group which usually controlled a complete theatre of operations, or a large segment of a large theatre. A signal regiment and extra staff units were usually under direct Army Group command and their functions were usually theatre-wide.

Plate 23: *Gen Rommel takes a tea break after the fall of Tobruk, conferring with a staff officer and with Afrika Korps HQ vehicles, including a radio van, marked in the background. Rommel appears to be wearing a rather scruffy leather overcoat while the staff officer wears greatcoat.*

For specific operations GHQ Troops (Heerstruppen) could be allocated to the higher commands from the GHQ pool. This comprised all armoured, artillery, engineer, signal, chemical warfare and other units not otherwise allotted to divisions. Some Luftwaffe ground and Flak units were included in the GHQ pool, also, and could be deployed under Army command.

There were, of course, no specific scales of deployment. Typical allocation of GHQ troops was to augment Corps and Armies during major offensives. For an Army Corps in the May 1940 invasion of France and Flanders the typical addition of GHQ troops was as follows: two artillery commanders and their staffs, two artillery regi-

mental HQs, two medium artillery battalic (105mm), four medium artillery battalic (150mm), two heavy artillery battalions (210mr two heavy artillery batteries (210mm), one hea artillery battalion (240mm), one heavy artille battalion (300mm), four heavy artillery batter (300mm), two artillery observation battalio three engineer bridging columns, one ex infantry battalion, one heavy anti-tank battali one light anti-tank battalion, one chemical w fare regimental HQ, one chemical warfare batt ion.

The strong emphasis on artillery, together w extra bridging columns, reflects the nature of t planning for the 1940 campaign.

INFANTRY DIVISION

The standard Infantry Division (Infanterie-Division) in the mid-war period comprised a divisional HQ, a reconnaissance battalion, three infantry regiments, an artillery regiment, an engi-

neer battalion, an antitank battalion, a signal b talion, and service units. The chain of comma is shown below:

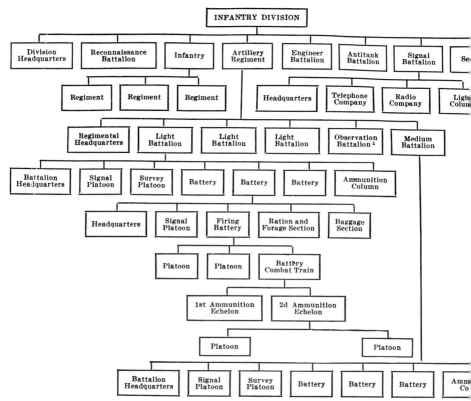

[1] The Observation Battalion was part of the GHQ pool.

The manpower and transport of an Infantry Division is shown in the table below. Key to abbreviations: O and EM — officers and enlisted men; Mtrcl — motorcycles; H-Dr — horse-drawn.

Units	O and EM	Mtrcl	Other Mtr Vehicles	H-Dr vehicles	Horses
Division headquarters	152	17	31		20
Reconnaissance battalion	575	35	30	3	213
Three infantry regiments	9,477	135	219	642	1,923
Artillery regiment	2,700	38	35	226	2,211
Engineer battalion	800	43	87	19	52
Antitank battalion	599	64	113		
Signal battalion	474	32	103	7	52
Services	2,200	98	325	30	218
TOTAL	16,977	462	943	927	4,689

The armament of an Infantry Division is shown in the following table.
Key to abbreviations: Rcn Bn — reconnaissance battalion; AT — anti-tank.

Weapons	Rcn Bn	3 Inf Regts	Arty Regt	AT Bn	Engr Bn	TOTAL
Machine pistols (excluding those in armoured cars)		432				432
Machine guns, light	24	345	24	18	27	444[1]
Machine guns, heavy	8	108				116
7.92mm anti-tank rifles		81			81	
20mm anti-tank guns				12		12
37mm anti-tank guns	3	36				39
50mm anti-tank guns				24		24
50mm mortars	3	81				84
81mm mortars	3	54				57
75mm infantry howitzers	2	18				20
180mm infantry howitzers		6				6
105mm gun howitzers			36			36
150mm gun howitzers			8			8
105mm guns			4			4

[1] Includes two in Div HQ and four in Div Sig Bn.

Plate 24: *The basic infantry unit was the platoon, comprising four rifle sections each with a machine gun. Here a platoon rests on the road to Oslo in April 1940, with the four MG34s lined-up and rifles piled. In front of the platoon is the company commander and the senior NCO, Der Spiess, with the twin band of braid on his cuffs. Note the MG34 folded tripods and the spare barrels in holders resting on top of the ammunition boxes. The rest of the company is in the background.*

Plate 25: *An infantry platoon takes cover in a ditch during the advance on Kiev in 1941. They are waiting for an artillery bombardment to lift before they move forward. Behind them Russian prisoners are being guarded.*

Plate 26: *The ubiquitous MG34 in action, mounted on its tripod in the 'heavy machine-gun' role. Note the rolled Zeltbahns on the belts, water bottle and bread bag. The gunner has a toolbox for the gun fitted to his belt. The black object behind the gun commander's helmet (right) is the lens cover for his Zeiss binoculars which has been pushed back out of the way on the neckstrap.*

Plate 27: *An infantry platoon on the march during the invasion of Russia in 1941. Note the helmets slung from belts. The Unteroffizier on the right has binoculars slung, and the Unteroffizier on the left has his anti-gas cape slung across his chest in its valise.*

Plate 28: *A complete rifle section moves down a French or Belgian village street during the May 1940 campaign in the west. They are probably from a panzer-division infantry element as they carry goggles for riding a half-track. An anti-gas cape is carried in the valise slung across the chest.*

Plate 29: *German troops enter Prague when the country was annexed in March 1939. Motorcycle troops were much favoured for reconnaissance units.*

The rear detail of the voluminous rubberised coat for motorcycle troops is well shown here. Note the anti-gas respirator slung across the body.

An increasingly important variation was the Motorised Infantry Division (Infanterie-Division (Mot.)) which differed from the ordinary infantry division in having all units motorised and no allocation of horses. There were only two infantry regiments instead of three. The artillery regiment was reduced to only two battalions of 105mm guns and there were two batteries of 150mm howitzers. There was also a motorcyc[] battalion, and in most cases a panzer (tank) ba[] talion was added, sometimes more. Typical ma[] power and equipment is shown in the tabl[] below. Key to abbreviations: Hv Armd C/L Arm[] C — heavy and light armoured cars; Pz.Kw - Panzerkampfwagen (tank); Mtz — motorised.

Units	O and EM	Mtrcl	Other Mtr vehicles	L Armd- C	Hv Armd- C	PzKw II	PzKw III	PzKw IV
Division headquarters	152	30	31					
Panzer battalion	649	50	86			7	37	10
Motorcycle battalion	1,055	271	121					
Panzer reconnaissance battalion	637	116	104	18	6			
Two motorised infantry regiments	6,190	590	1,164					
Motorised artillery regiment	1,835	125	335					
Motorised engineer battalion	862	58	133					
Anti-tank battalion	599	64	113					
Motorised signal battalion	474	32	103					
Services	1,866	108	371					
TOTAL	14,319	1,453	2,561	18	6	7	37	10

Weapons	Panzer Bn	Mtrcl Bn	Panzer Rcn Bn	2Mtz Inf Regts	Mtz Arty Regt	Mtz Engr Bn	AT Bn	Mtz Sig Bn	TOTAL
Machine guns, light	99	58	51	236	18	27	18	4	511
Machine guns, heavy		14	2	72					88
Anti-tank rifles		9	3	54					66
20mm tank guns	7		10				12		29
50mm tank guns	37								37
75mm tank guns	10								10
37mm anti-tank guns				24					24
50mm anti-tank guns	3	3			24				30
50mm motors		9	3	54					66
81mm motors	6		36						42
75mm infantry howitzers		2	2	12					16
150mm infantry howitzers				4					4
105mm guns					4				4
150mm gun-howitzers					8				8
105mm gun-howitzers					24				24

PANZER DIVISION

The Armoured Division (Panzer-Division) existed in several different forms but a typical formation and chain of command is shown in the table opposite:
In earlier establishments the motorcycle battalion was absent and its place was occupied by a reconnaissance battalion which could have com[] prised the PzKpfw I light tank and/or ligh[] armoured cars with a motorcycle element.
The manpower, vehicles and equipment o[] Panzer Division organised as in the table ar[] shown in the two tables below:

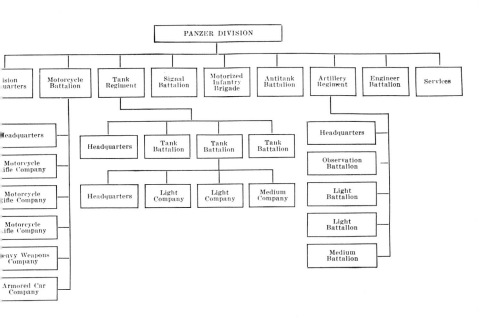

Units	O and EM	Mtrcl	Other Mtr vehicles	Lt Armd-C	Hv Armd-C	PzKw II	PzKw III	PzKw IV
Division headquarters	185	39	31					
Panzer regiment	2,416	170	353			28	114	30
Motorcycle battalion	1,153	236	150	18	6			
Motorized infantry brigade	4,409	314	713					
Panzer artillery regiment	2,102	132	455					
Panzer engineer battalion	979	101	220			2		
Antitank battalion	552	44	93					
Panzer signal battalion	420	27	85					
Services	2,157	120	446					
TOTAL	14,373	1,183	2,546	18	6	30	114	30

Weapons	Panzer Regt	Mtrcl Bn	Mtz Inf Brig	Panzer Arty Regt	Panzer Engr Bn	AT Bn	Panzer Sig Bn	TOTAL
Machine pistols			156				156	
Machine guns, light	376	87	358	24	48	16	22	931
Machine guns, heavy	24	12	48				84	
Anti-tank rifles		9	36				45	
20mm AA/AT guns	28	18			2	12		60
37mm anti-tank guns			18					18
50mm tank guns	106							106
50mm anti-tank guns		3	18			18		39
81mm mortars		6	24					30
75mm infantry howitzers	30	2	16					48
150mm infantry howitzers			8					8
105mm gun-howitzers				24				24
105mm guns				4				4
150mm gun-howitzers				8				8

41

MOUNTAIN DIVISION

The Mountain Division (Gebirgs-Division) was usually a more simple organisation, typically comprising a divisional HQ, a bicycle battalion, two mountain infantry regiments, a mountain artillery regiment (pack howitzers), a mountain engineer battalion, an anti-tank battalion, mountain signal battalion and service units. The tables below show the typical manpower, veh cles and equipment.

Units	O and EM	Mtrcl	Other Mtr vehicles	H-Dr vehicles	Horses or mules
Division headquarters	200	12	26		20
Bicycle battalion	551	57	37		
Two mountain infantry regiments	6,506	168	270	348	950
Mountain artillery regiment	2,500	12	23	178	1,785
Mountain engineer battalion	1,049	42	96	64	256
Anti-tank battalion	599	64	113		
Mountain signal battalion	476	28	102	7	56
Services	2,250	64	191	117	439
TOTAL	14,131	447	858	714	3,506

Weapons	Bcl Bn	Mtn Inf Regts	Mtn Arty Regt	Mtn Engr Bn	AT Bn	Mtn Sig Bn	TOTAL
Machine guns, light	24	356	24	27	18	4	453
Machine guns, heavy	8	84					92
Anti-tank rifles		72					72
20mm AA/AT guns					12		12
37mm anti-tank guns	3	24					27
50mm anti-tank guns					24		24
50mm mortars	6	54					60
81mm mortars	3	36					39
75mm mtn howitzers	2	12	36				50
105mm gun-howitzers			12				12

Plate 30: *Men of a Mountain Division deploying up to the 'winter line' in Italy in late 1943. They are wearing the reversible anorak, camouflage side outwards. This photograph was taken in Abruzzi province.*

30

LIGHT DIVISION

The Light Division (Jäger-Division or Leichte-Division) was found in some theatres of war, notably North Africa. The establishment was very variable but was most similar to a Motorised Infantry Division. Most had two infantry regiments, one artillery regiment which might be motorised with assault guns, a reconnaissance or bicycle battalion and usual support units.

DIVISIONAL AND TACTICAL SIGNS

Military markings in any detail are beyond the scope of this book due to the complexity of the subject, but mention is made here just for completeness. Divisions had distinctive signs of a geometric, runic, or heraldic nature. A classic example of the latter was the 'Berlin Bear' of 3.Panzer-Division which reflected its recruiting base and headquarters in Berlin. The elite 'Gross Deutschland' Division had the outline of a steel helmet, PanzerLehr a gothic 'L', 7 Panzer-Division a 'Y' and so on. These were usually carried on fronts and rears of vehicles and could also be seen on related route boards and sign boards, etc.

A very neat system of tactical signs was used on maps and charts to indicate precise units within a division in shorthand form. Thus there was a sign for an armoured car company, a tank company, towed artillery, signals unit, etc, drawn in outline form. The tank unit was indicated by a 'lozenge' shape, for example. Numbers alongside indicated the individual unit. A modified form of the sign was also carried on vehicles front and rear. This assisted convoy controllers, command staff, military police, etc, to identify units on the march. However, in frontline areas the signs of all types on vehicles were frequently obliterated by mud or paint for security reasons and they were not always used in any case. A tactical number system was used on tanks which indicated by the combination of numbers the company and platoon of the individual vehicle. This usually took the form of a prominent three-digit display on the turret or superstructure, but in the prewar and early war period removable small 'lozenge'-shaped number boards (matching the tactical sign for a tank) were often carried instead on the tank's superstructure.

Plate 31: Top row: *Examples of divisional signs (from left) 7th Panzer Division (1940), Gross Deutschland, 20th Panzer Division (1940), 1st Panzer Division (1939).*
Bottom Row: *Examples of tactical signs (from left) SP gun, armoured car, motorised infantry and tank. The latter was rarely carried on tanks, but was marked on the wheeled transport of tank units.*

31

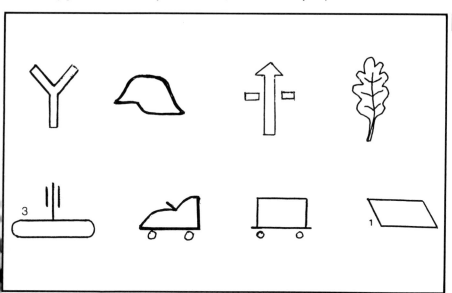

DEUTSCHER VOLKSSTURM

As the Allies closed in on the German homeland in late 1944, it was decided to form the Deutscher Volkssturm (German People's Militia) which was, in effect, a German equivalent to the British Home Guard. Its formation was announced in a broadcast by Hitler on 18 October 1944, and it came into being on 20 October. The actual organisation was instituted on 25 September 1944. Though officially part of the Wehrmacht, the administration was done through Nazi Party (NDSAP) resources. This was due to its local town nature and as there existed the party organisation linked to all areas of the country, party Gauleiters were made commanders of units corresponding to the network of Nazi Party branches. Overall control was vested in Heinrich Himmler who was commander of the replacement army (reserves) among his many other state appointments.

Every man from 16-60 not already in th armed forces had to register for the Volkssturm Training was given on one evening a week. Th organisation roughly matched that of an infantr battalion at local level. Members were respons ble for providing their own arms and uniform though there were local appeals and a certai amount of scavenging from official sources t help out. Arms were scarce and much assortec The only common item was an armband for th left arm and though some men wore only civilia dress with the armband, others were furnishe with a variety of cast-off political and militar uniform items.

There were 43 Gau administrations for th Volkssturm, each with numerous battalior under command depending on the area, wit very many more, of course, in densely populate areas. The Volkssturm also took under comman a number of Standschützen battalions forme from long-established local rifle associations th had traditionally flourished in the Tyrol area both German and Austrian borders. An unusu unit, also taken under Volkssturm command, w Freikorps Sauerland, which was a local defen organisation set up on local Gau initiative Westphalia some time before the Volksstur itself was instituted.

The Volkssturm remained organised only to battalion level, with the usual breakdown in companies and platoons. It was not at any tin grouped into brigades or divisions.

Plate 32: *Deutscher Volkssturm men parade in Berli in November 1944. Most are in civilian clothing, but some have uniforms.*

WOMEN AUXILIARIES

Prewar planners had not considered a women's branch for the Heer and it was not until after the 1940 campaign in the west, when a huge area of Europe was occupied, that it was realised that women could carry out office and administration work to release men for combat duties. The first women's branch established was a Corps of Army Signal Auxiliaries (Nachrichtenhelferinnen des Heeres) on 1 October 1940. Some nurses from the German Red Cross (Deutsche Rot Kreuz) joined as a nucleus and volunteers were recruited. All were trained in signals and communications work for headquarters and command service.

In October 1941 a second branch was formed, the Corps of Welfare Auxiliaries (Betreungshelferinnenschaft). They took over all military welfare work, some of which had been pre-

viously carried out on behalf of the Heer German Red Cross personnel who were absorb into the new arm. The Welfare Auxiliari provided similar services to the British W and included in their duties service to civilia in occupied areas, such as bombed-out famili etc.

On 27 February 1942 a Corps of Staff Aux iaries (Stabshelferinnenschaft) was establish for clerical and secretarial duties. Some Sign Auxiliaries who were already carrying out th tasks transferred to the new branch and othe were recruited to make up the establishment.

The final Heer branch to be formed, in 194 was a Corps of Women Horse Breakers (Bere erinnen) for service at equestrian schools a depots where they were specifically employed the training of remounts and young horses.

33

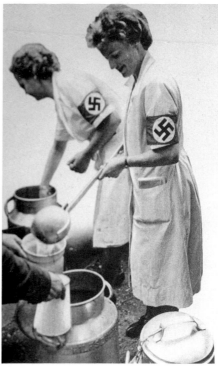

Plate 33: *Women Signal Auxiliaries in service dress, showing the signallers' 'Blitz' specialist badge on the left arm and left side of the Feldmütze.*

Plate 34: *Women Signal Auxiliaries with male colleagues operating the Heer's Paris telephone exchange. They are wearing the light grey or light brown overall work dress over the light blue work shirt. The woman at the right wears the 'Blitz' metal brooch on her black tie, in accordance with the regulations for its wear.*

Plate 35: *Women Welfare Auxiliaries serve milk to bombed-out French civilians. They wear the medical-type white coat from German Red Cross supplies plus a swastika armband, black stockings and shoes.*

45

A logical step was taken on 29 November 1944 when an order was made forming the Corps of Women Armed Forces Auxiliaries (Wehrmachthelferinnenkorps) as one overall administration with common ranks for all women's branches of the Heer, the Kriegsmarine and the Luftwaffe. However, the various branches all continued to wear their particular uniforms and distinctions. The army auxiliaries were then known as Wehrmachthelferinnen (Heer) — Armed Forces Auxiliaries (Army).

The age range for recruits to the women's auxiliaries was 18-40. Though early recruits were all volunteers, from December 1941 women witho family commitments were liable for conscriptie and could be directed to the Auxiliary service, other war work. A plan drawn up late in 19 proposed to make greater use of women's aux iaries and called for an extra 150,000 conscrip in 1945. On 7 May 1945, the day before the fo mal German surrender to the Allies, the Aux iary services were officially disbanded and all t women were immediately discharged, thus ob ating the problem of dealing with large numbe of women prisoners-of-war which would ha otherwise faced the Allies.

SMALL ARMS

A full coverage of German small arms in beyond the scope of this book, but for identification purposes, and because they figure in most photographs of German troops in action, the most commonly used weapons are detailed here.

Karbine 98 Kurz (Kar 98K) Mauser
Calibre: 7.92mm (.312in); *magazine capacity*: 5 rounds; *weight*: 8lb 8oz; *range*: 3,000yd (max); 800yd (effective). This was the standard rifle most often seen in use.

Pistole 1938 (P38) Walther
Calibre: 9mm (.354in); *magazine capacity*: 8 rounds; *weight*: 2lb 1/2oz empty; *range*: 1,150yd (max), 25yd (effective).

Pistole 1908 (P08) Luger
Calibre: 9mm (.354in); *magazine capacity*: 8 rounds, *weight*: 1lb 14oz empty; other details as for the P38. The P38 and P08 were the two most commonly used pistols, carried in holsters on the belt

Maschinenpistole 38 und 40 (MP38 and MP40)
Calibre: 9mm (.354in); *magazine capacity*: 32 rounds in detachable box magazine; *weight*: 1 7oz loaded; *range*: 1,850yd (max), 200yd (eff tive); *rate of fire*; up to 100rpm burst fire. Th were the two most commonly used sub-machi guns, differing from each other only in sm details. This was the weapon most often carri by platoon and section leaders. Also to be se with some second line units was the earl Bergmann MP34 sub-machine gun which ha wooden stock, a side box magazine and a pe rated barrel sleeve.

Maschinengewehr 34 (MG34)
Calibre: 7.92mm; *weight*: 26lb 8oz; *ran 5,000yd (max), 3,825 yd, tripod mounted (eff tive), 2,000yds bipod mounted (effective); *rate fire*: up to 900rpm

Maschinengewehr 42 (MG42)
Calibre: 7.92mm; *weight*: 25lb 8oz; *range*: as MG34; *rate of fire*: 1,300rpm (decrease in ac racy compared to MG34). The MG34 and

Plate 36: *The MP38.*

Plate 37: *The StuG 44.*

er, simplified, MG42 were the standard issue achine guns of the Wehrmacht. They could be ed in the 'heavy' role on a folding tripod ount, and in the 'light' role on a fitted bipod. ley could also be used in the anti-aircraft role. le MG34 had both semi- and fully automatic tion and a recoil booster. The MG42, which ver fully supplanted the MG34, was produced in the later part of World War 2 and the design was modified to make production easier. It had only fully automatic action. Both weapons were air-cooled and had a barrel-changing facility.

Plate 38: *The MG42 showing its features.*

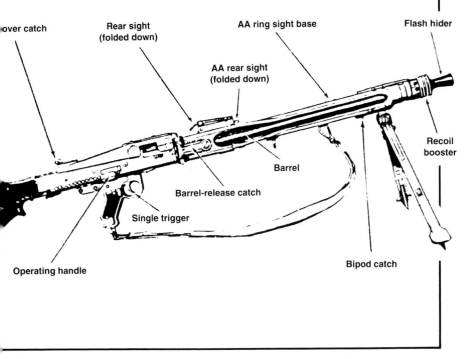

over catch

Rear sight
(folded down)

AA ring sight base

Flash hider

AA rear sight
(folded down)

Recoil
booster

Barrel

Barrel-release catch

Single trigger

Bipod catch

Operating handle

Sturmgewehr 44 (StG44)

Calibre: 7.92mm; *weight*: 11lb 8oz; *magazine capacity*: 30 rounds selective fire. This was an important type designed in the early part of World War 2 as a replacement for both the rifle and the sub-machine gun. To simplify production much use was made of simple metal pressings. It could take a bayonet and a grenade launcher. It entered production in mid-1943 originally designated MP43 but changed to MP44 in April 1944. In December 1944 the designation was changed from MP (Maschinen pistole) to Sturmgewehr (assault rifle) seemingly at Hitler's suggestion as this more truly described its function. Because it was heavy a lighter version, the StG45, was being tested as a prototype when the war ended. Both guns had a big influence on postwar assault rifles which copied many of their features. Over 60,000 StG44s were produced and they were mainly issued to elite fighting units.

Plate 39: *MG34 machine-gun team deploying (drawing by Shin Udea, Tamiya Co).*

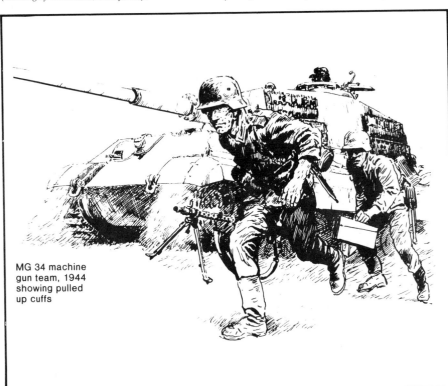

MG 34 machine gun team, 1944 showing pulled up cuffs

39

3. Uniforms and Insignia

Throughout the period of the Third Reich the basic colour of the German Army service dress was field grey (Feldgrau) and this was a continuation of the same drab colour introduced for the Kaiser's army in 1910 (after troop trials which started in 1907). This colour replaced the dark blue which had long been the service dress colour of the Prussian and German armies.

Despite its name, field grey is actually a shade of green, best described as green with a greyish tinge. Field grey was also extensively used as a paint colour and almost all metal items, such as helmets, canisters, bicycles and vehicles (except where otherwise camouflaged) were so painted.

The other colour most used in uniforms of the tropical or lightweight type was rush green or reed green and this also had some ancestry, being the colour used for the linen helmet covers first issued in 1892 for field use. However, there was more variety than this generalisation implies, and variations are noted in the text.

The standard uniforms introduced and worn during the Third Reich period were characterised by a balanced combination of functional design and a smart appearance and finish. The quality was excellent but there was a marked falling off

in standard from 1942 onwards as drast economies were made. Wartime economies, to forced actual changes in service dress design save material. Whereas the enlisted man's wo service dress contained 20% rayon mixed with in 1939, the uniforms made from 1943 on ha 50% or even less, wool content and the woo itself was often low grade recycled material.

Throughout the Third Reich period there wa some variation in the actual shade of field gre colour, both in clothing material and pai shades, and this shade variation was further con pounded by wear, washing and weathering. was therefore not unusual for, say, trousers an tunic not to match exactly in shade and th point should be borne in mind when interpretin from photographs, collecting uniform garment or modelling German soldiers. There were man exceptions to the rules and some of these a illustrated.

Badges, insignia and ranks in general followe the designations, styles and traditions that date back to the days of the Kaiser's army or earlie However, there were new badges and awards in tiated in the Third Reich era which were uniqu to the period.

ARMY RANKS

The table on page 51 gives a concise listing of all the army ranks most commonly encountered. The ranks matched quite closely with British and American equivalents which are given in the table for comparison. In some cases, however, the equivalents are approximate rather than precise. The table shows designations as in 1943. The following notes should be read in conjunction with the table:

1. The Generalfeldmarschall rank was not introduced in the Third Reich era until 20 April 1936 (Hitler's birthday), though it had been used prior to 1918.

2. In addition to the generals' ranks for the main fighting arms given in the table there were designations for generals in various support services, such as Generalveterinar (Veterinary General), Generalarzt (Medical General)

3. The same applied to field and company officer ranks. Thus there was also the rank of Oberstarzt (Medical Colonel) and Stabsarzt (Medical Captain). Directors of Music also had distinctive titles — Obermusikmeister (Lieutenant), Stabsmusikmeister (Captain), Musikinspizient (Inspector of Music — Major), Obermusikinspizient (Senior Inspector of Music — Colonel). Though dressed in officer style, the music branch was considered a specialisation of its own and Directors of Music were not classed as officers.

4. The traditional rank of Rittmeister was used instead of Hauptmann (captain) in cavalry and other horsed units)

5. Fähnrich was a distinctive rank title given an officer candidate. He served in the junio and senior NCO ranks and in ordinary se vice dress was distinguished by twin silv braids across the outer end of his should straps. He could also wear officer's silv cords on his peaked service cap and an off cers' silver side arm tassel (Portepee).

6. The title of Grenadier for a private in th infantry was introduced by Hitler in Noven ber 1942, reviving a traditional name fro the time of Frederick the Great. Previous this an infantry private was designated Schütze. Infantrymen in armoured division who were previously ranked Panzerschütz were consequently ranked Panzer-Grenadie All infantry regiments from this time we known as Grenadier-Regimenter, but moun tain regiments and rifle troop battalion (Jäger-Bataillonen) were unaffected by thes changes so a rifleman retained the rank Schütze. Two other special designation encountered for privates were Musketie unique to some infantry units within Panz Korps 'Gross Deutschland', and Fusilier, i regiments titled as Fusilier regiments.

7. NCO candidates (Unteroffizieranwärter) wo a single silver braid across the outer end the shoulder strap, similar in style to t twin braids of an officer candidate (see no 5 above). The braid could be stitched

German Army Rank	Translation	Corresponding US Army rank (according to function)	Corresponding British Army rank
Generalfeldmarschall	General Field Marshal	None	Field Marshal
Generaloberst	Colonel General	General	General
General der Infanterie	General of Infantry	Lieutenant-General	Lieutenant-General
Artilleri	Artillery		
Kavallerie	Cavalry		
Pioniere	Engineers		
Panzertruppe, etc.	Armoured Troops, etc		
Generalleutnant	Lieutenant-General	Major-General	Major-General
Generalmajor	Major-General	Brigadier-General	Brigadier
Oberst	Colonel	Colonel	Colonel
Oberstleutnant	Lieutenant-Colonel	Lieutenant-Colonel	Lieutenant-Colonel
Major	Major	Major	Major
Hauptmann	Captain	Captain	Captain
Rittmeister	Captain of Cavalry		
Oberleutnant	First Lieutenant	First Lieutenant	Lieutenant
Leutnant	Lieutenant	Second Lieutenant	Second Lieutenant
Stabsfeldwebel	Staff Sergeant	Master Sergeant	Staff Sergeant Major
Stabswachtmeister	Staff Cavalry Sergeant	Regimental Sergeant Major	
Stabsfeuerwerker	Staff Ordnance Sergeant		
Wallstabsfeldwebel	Staff Fort Sergeant		
Festungspionierstabsfeldwebel	Staff Fortification Engineer Sergeant		
Stabsfunkmeister	Staff Radio Sergeant		
Stabsbrieftaubenmeister	Staff Carrier Pigeon Sergeant		
Stabsschirrmeister	Staff Maintenance Sergeant		
Hauptfeldwebel	Chief Sergeant	First Sergeant	Regimental Sergeant Major
Hauptwachtmeister	Chief Cavalry Sergeant		
Oberfeldwebel	First Sergeant	Master Sergeant	Battalion Sergeant Major
Oberwachtmeister	First Cavalry Sergeant		
Oberfähnrich	Ensign (Officer Candidate)		
Oberfeuerwerker	First Ordnance Sergeant		
Walloberfeldwebel	First Fort Sergeant		
Festungspionieroberfeldwebel	First Fortification: Engineer Sergeant		
Oberfunkmeister	First Radio Sergeant		
Oberbrieftaubenmeister	First Carrier Pigeon: Sergeant		
Oberschirrmeister	First Maintenance: Sergeant		
Feldwebel	Sergeant	Technical Sergeant	Company Sergeant Major
Wachtmeister	Cavalry Sergeant		
Feuerwerker	Ordnance Sergeant		
Wallfeldwebel	Fort Sergeant		
Festungspionierfeldwebel	Fortification Engineer: Sergeant		
Funkmeister	Radio Sergeant		
Brieftaubenmeister	Carrier Pigeon Sergeant		
Schirrmeister	Mantenance Sergeant		
Fähnrich	Officer Candidate		
Unterfeldwebel	Junior Sergeant	Staff Sergeant	Sergeant
Unterwachtmeister	Junior Cavalry Sergeant		
Unteroffizier, Fahnenfunker-Unteroffizier	Junior NCO	Sergeant	Lance Sergeant
Stabsgefreiter	Staff Lance Corporal		
Obergefreiter	Chief Lance Corporal	Corporal	Corporal
Gefreiter, Fahnenjunker-Gefreiter	Lance Corporal Junior Cadet	Acting Corporal	Lance Corporal
Obergrenadier	Chief Infantryman	Private First Class	Senior Private
Oberjäger	Chief Chasseur		
Oberreiter	Chief Cavalryman		
Oberkanonier	Chief Gunner		
Oberpionier	Chief Engineer		
Oberfunker	Chief Radioman		
Oberfahrer	Chief Driver		
Oberkraftfahrer	Chief Motor Driver		
Grenadier	Infantryman	Private	Private
Jäger	Chasseur		
Reiter	Cavalryman		Trooper
Kanonier	Gunner		Gunner
Funker	Radioman		Signalman
Fahrer	Driver (horse transport)		
Kraftfahrer	Motor Driver		Driver
Pionier	Engineer		Sapper
Schültze	Rifleman		Rifleman

51

The national emblem, worn on the right breast of tunics in all orders of dress (but not camouflage clothing) was an eagle badge, the Hoheitzabzeichen, which was woven in silver-white thread on a very dark bottle green backing. On the tropical dress, however, as worn in North Africa, the same emblem was in grey on a light tan cloth backing (see back cover). For colonels the emblem was woven in silver and for generals it was woven in gold, again on a tan background for North Africa.

On forage caps the Hoheitzabzeichen was worn on the front above a national cockade (Reichskokarde) of red/white/black, the old Imperial German national colours. On the peaked service cap the Hoheitzabzeichen was carried above the Reichskokarde which had an oakleaf surround.

Plate 40: *Army pattern Hoheitzabzeichen, worn on right breast.*

Plate 41: *Hoheitzabzeichen with Reichskokarde in oakleaf surround as worn on the peaked service cap, colour silver, with cockade in national colours.*

Plate 42: *Helmet insignia transfers, shown on the Model 1916 helmet.*

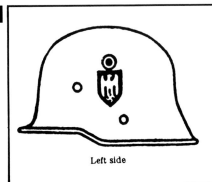

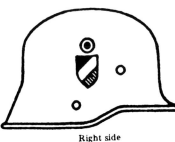

Left side

Right side

In the last two years of World War 2 when ⌐terials were in short supply, an inferior qual- Hoheitzabzeichen was issued, printed or ⌐broidered on a dark grey cloth background ⌐ich was cut, or more often folded in a simple ⌐ngular shape, apex downwards and stitched place.

The Hoheitzabzeichen was introduced in ⌐ruary 1934 and the Reichskokarde for head- ⌐ar was introduced in March 1933.

The steel helmet (Stahlhelm) had its own ⌐ique markings. On the right side was carried a ⌐eld transfer divided diagonally into the ⌐tional colours of black/white/red (in that order, ⌐ to bottom), and on the left side was a shield transfer featuring the stylised Wehrmacht silver eagle on a black background. The shield in national colours was discontinued during 1940 and the eagle transfer was discarded shortly afterwards. New or repainted helmets were thereafter finished in plain colours. However, there were many variations from standard. Prewar photographs of 1938-39 show helmets lacking the transfers on occasion. The transfers often wore off and left only a partial impression and sometimes they were deliberately painted over or scratched off as they could provide an aiming mark for a sniper. Conversely it was possible to see helmets up to 1945 that still had the transfers in place.

WAFFENFARBEN — ARM OF SERVICE COLOURS

⌐he arm of service (or branch) was indicated by a ⌐nge of colours known as Waffenfarben (which short for Waffengatungsfarbe which means ⌐rm of service colour'). This had been a tradi- ⌐onal means of showing the branch on German ⌐my uniforms for many years. In the form used ⌐ the Third Reich era it was derived from the ⌐heme introduced for the Kaiser's army in ⌐eptember 1915. This was continued by the post- ⌐919 Reichsheer, the major change in the Third ⌐eich era being only the introduction of more ⌐olours as branches proliferated. In a simpler ⌐rm Waffenfarben had been used by the German ⌐rmy back in the 19th century.

Waffenfarben was worn in the form of ⌐oloured piping round the should straps (addi- ⌐onal to any rank or unit insignia) and on forage ⌐aps in the form of an inverted chevron pattern ⌐bove the Reichskokarde. The collar of the army ⌐unic featured a twin bar of woven silver-grey ⌐hread, the whole being incorporated on a back- ⌐ng patch. A central strip in each bar was woven ⌐ the Waffenfarbe colour, this style of lace being ⌐nown as Doppelitze. After 1940 these colour ⌐trips were discarded and the bars remained ⌐lain silver-grey. Officers wore silver braid and ⌐any retained the Doppelitze after 1940 on uni- ⌐orms purchased from military tailors. In the lat- ⌐er part of the war, particularly in conjunction ⌐vith the 1943 and 1944 pattern tunics, an infe- ⌐ior type of collar patch was issued which con- ⌐isted of grey woven bars on thin grey cloth back- ⌐ng.

The collar of the original service tunic was faced in dark bottle green cloth and officers wore Waffenfarbe as an edging to the collar. Senior NCOs (of unteroffizier rank and above) wore a 9mm wide silver-grey braid round the edge of the service dress collar. On the 1943 and 1944 pattern tunics, the dark bottle green facing material was often omitted for economy, and lacing and Waffenfarbe, appropriate to rank, were worn directly on the plain field grey collar.

Prior to the outbreak of war in September 1939 the Waffenfarbe on the shoulder strap was quite often closely related to other distinctions related to the branch or arm of service. In some cases these distinctions (in the form of letters or monograms) were retained in wartime, but in most cases they were removed for security reasons and only the Waffenfarbe remained, together with rank distinction, on the shoulder strap. An example was infantry regiment 'Gross Deutschland', an elite unit, whose shoulder straps carried a stylised GD monogram together with the white Waffenfarbe to indicate infantry. For part of the war, at least, the distinction on the shoulder strap was retained, from pictorial evidence, but a more typical case would be an ordinary infantry regiment. In peacetime the number of the regiment was carried on the shoulder strap, but after the outbreak of war it was removed to give a plain strap with only the white Waffenfarbe retained.

SHOULDER STRAPS

⌐he shoulder strap was an important part of the ⌐erman army uniform. It not only indicated arm ⌐f service, by the Waffenfarbe, but also carried ⌐he rank distinctions and unit identification, though as already noted the latter was largely discontinued after the start of World War 2.

Rank was always designated on shoulder straps, though junior NCOs also wore arm badges. These are shown in the accompanying diagrams, as are the styles of shoulder strap rank designations. Privates and junior NCOs had plain shoulder straps decorated only with the appropriate Waffenfarbe. Unteroffiziers (junior sergeants) had an open-ended braid decoration while all other NCOs had a full braid surround, 9mm wide, sewn immediately inside the Waffenfarbe piping. Also on the shoulder strap was the cypher, monogram, or regimental number as appropriate. Some regiments also had 'tradition' badges carried over as a vestige from Imperial German Army days. For example the 5th Cavalry had a small 'death's head' device having formerly been a 'Death's Head Hussar' regiment. The shoulder strap button also usually carried a number indicating the company, squadron or platoon within the unit. From September 1939 the buttons were usually plain in line with the removal of the regimental identification devices.

Shoulder straps were detachable for cleaning and were not always worn. Like the collar they were faced with dark bottle green material. However, the 1943 and 1944 pattern tunics were issued without the facing material on the shoulder straps and the Waffenfarbe and distinc were affixed direct to the field grey material. original pattern of shoulder strap had a pointed end, but in 1938-39 a shoulder strap rounded end was introduced. The older ty shoulder strap was still to be seen, however, into World War 2.

Officers' shoulder straps were in silver being either edged with, or backed by (m and above), the Waffenfarbe. Until the outb of war unit identity devices were carrie described for enlisted men.

On the tropical uniform worn in North A the facing material was tan instead of dark b green and copper-coloured yarn replaced th ver-grey braid. However, pictorial evidence gests that the shoulder straps of the standard vice dress were sometimes worn with the tro tunic.

The following table lists the Waffent colours and is linked to the accompanying which shows the related shoulder strap dev for various units and branches of service. The ures in brackets in the table correspond to diagrams in the shoulder strap plate

TABLE OF WAFFENFARBEN

Arm of service	Colours	Shoulder straps
Generals (Generale)	Bright red (hochrot)	No numbers
General headquarters of armed forces (Oberkommando der Wehrmacht)	Carmine red (karmesin rot)	No numbers
General headquarters of army (Oberkommando des Heeres)	Carmine red	No numbers
War Department and General Staff (Reichskriegsministerium und Generalstab)	Carmine red	No numbers
Army group headquarters (Heeresgruppenkommando)	White (weiss)	'G' and Arabic number (1)
Army corps headquarters (Generalkommando)	White	Roman number of corps (2)
Infantry division headquarters (Infanterie-Divisionsstab)	White	'D' and number of division (3
Armoured division headquarters (Panzer-Divisionsstab)	Pink (rosa)	'D' and number of Division (4
Anti-tank battalions of armoured division (Panzerjäger-Abteilungen der Panzer-Division)	Pink	'P' and number of battalion (5
Armoured train (Eisenbahn-Panzer-Zug)	Pink	'E' (6)
Infantry regiments (Infanterie-Regimenter)	White	Number of regiment (7)
Mountain Jäger Regiments and Jäger Battalions, Infantry (Gebirgsjägerregimenter und Jägerbataillone)	Light green (hellgrün)	Number of regiment (8)
Infantry Regiment 'Greater Germany' (Infanterieregiment 'Gross-Deutschland')	White	'GD' (9)
Guard Battalion 'Vienna' (Wachbataillon 'Wien')	White	'W' (10)
Machine-gun battalion (Maschinengewehrbataillon)	White	'M' and number of battalion (1
Parachute units, infantry (Fallschirmjäger-Einheiten)	White	'FJ' (12)
Reconnaissance regiments or battalions, infantry (Aufklärungsregimenter und -abteilungen)	Golden yellow (goldgelb)	'A' and number of regiment or batallion (13)
Cavalry and horse regiments (Kavallerie- und Reiterregimenter)	Golden yellow	Number of regiment (14)
Bicycle battalions (Radfahrer-Abteilungen)	Golden yellow	'R' and number of battalion (1
Artillery regiments (Artillerieregimenter)	Bright red (hochrot)	Number of regiment (16)
Horse-drawn artillery regiments (Berittene Artillerieregimenter)	Bright red	'R' and number of unit (17)
Observation battalions (Beobachtungsabteilungen)	Bright red	'B' and number of unit (18)
Smoke units (Nebelabteilungen)	Violet (violet)	'N' and number of battalion (1
Panzer reconnaissance units of Panzer or motorised division (Panzer-Aufklärungs-Abteilungen der motorisierten oder Panzer-division)	Copper brown (kupferbraun)	'A' and number of unit (20)
Motorcycle battalion in armoured division (Kraftradschützenbataillone)	Grass green (grasgrün)	'K' and number of unit (21)
Engineer battalions (Pionierbataillone)	Black (schwarz)	Number of battalion (22)

Arm of service	Colours	Shoulder straps
Fortress engineers (Festungspioniere)	Black	Gothic 'Fp' if unit existed in peacetime. Latin 'F' if formed on or after mobilisation (23)
Fortress engineer commander (Festungspionierkommandeur) Rank of regimental commander	Black	Gothic 'Fp' Roman numeral in Wehrkreis
Fortress engineer headquarters (Festungspionierstab)	Black	Gothic 'Fp' or Latin 'F' plus Arabic numbers 1-50
Signal battalions (Nachrichtenabteilungen)	Lemon yellow (zitronengelb)	Number of battalion (24)
Transportation battalions (Kraftfahr- und Fahrabteilungen)	Light blue (hellblau)	Number of battalion (25)
Medical battalions (Sanitätsabteilungen)	Cornflower blue (kornblumenblau)	Number of division (26)
Veterinary units (Veterinärabteilungen)	Carmine red	Number of division (27)
Chaplains (Heeresgeistliche)	Violet	No shoulder straps
Field signal command (Feldnachrichtenkommandantur)	Lemon yellow	Latin 'K' (28)
Anti-aircraft battalions (Flak-Bataillone)	White	Gothic 'Fl'
Military police (Feldgendarmerie)	Orange (orange)	No number. Nazi eagle and swastika surrounded by oak wreath on upper left arm; brown band with 'Feldgendarmerie' in silver inscribed on lower left arm
Local defence units (landesschützen-Einheiten)	White	Latin 'L' plus Arabic number of regiment or battalion
Some local defence units (Einige Landesschützen-Einheiten)	Light green	
Construction units (Bau-Einheiten)	Light brown (hellbraun)	
Railway engineers (Eisenbahnpioniere)	Black	Latin 'E' and Arabic numeral of unit
Administration of ordnance stores—enlisted men (Feldzeugkommando)	Light blue	Latin 'Fz' (29)
Officials (Beamten)	Dark green (dunkelgrün)	(30)
All (wartime)	All	Appearance with all devices removed (30)

43

21 22 23 24 25 26 27 28 29 30

11 12 13 14 15 16 17 18 19 20

1 2 3 4 5 6 7 8 9 10

TEMPORARY SLIP-ON SHOULDER STRAPS

In certain circumstances, such as temporary assignment to a particular unit or for home service, slip-on bands carrying regimental or unit numbers were worn over the uniform shoulder strap. In addition, the twin lace bars indicating a Fähnrich (officer candidate) or the single lace bars of a NCO candidate were often worn in the form of slip-on straps over the shoulder straps, particularly in the war years. Originally, however, they were stitched to the outer end of the shoulder strap. There were also plain slip-on covers in field grey worn by some officers to conceal the prominent braid of their shoulder straps in combat areas.

As noted above, badges of rank for both NCOs and officers were incorporated in the shoulder straps. The exception to this was the rank of private, for which the shoulder straps were plain, and junior NCOs whose rank was indicated by diamonds and/or chevrons on the upper sleeves of the service tunic. The chevrons and diamonds were woven in silver-grey or light grey for service dress, originally on dark bottle green backing.

The chevrons were 9mm wide. For tropical dre they were woven in copper brown on a tan bac ing. Later in World War 2 field grey backi material replaced the dark bottle green and the were variations in black backing (for the spec tank crew uniforms) and white (for the den working dress). From 1942-43 the Stabsgefrei chevrons were also worn by an Obergefreit and until 1936 an Oberschütze wore a sing

44 ENLISTED MEN

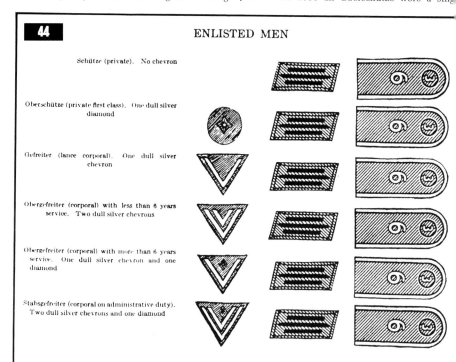

Schütze (private). No chevron

Oberschütze (private first class). One dull silver diamond

Gefreiter (lance corporal). One dull silver chevron

Obergefreiter (corporal) with less than 6 years service. Two dull silver chevrons

Obergefreiter (corporal) with more than 6 years service. One dull silver chevron and one diamond

Stabsgefreiter (corporal on administrative duty). Two dull silver chevrons and one diamond

Plates 44, 45, 46, 56 and 57 are reproduced from official US Army diagrams.

Company officers.

Leutnant (second lieutenant).
Lowest ranking officer. No
stars on shoulder straps

Oberleutnant (first lieutenant).
Shoulder strap has one gold
star

Hauptmann (Rittmeister in the
cavalry) (captain). Two gold
stars on shoulder straps

Field officers.

Major (major). Shoulder strap
has no star

Oberstleutnant (lieutenant colonel). One gold star on
shoulder strap

Oberst (colonel). Two gold
stars on shoulder strap

 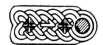

GENERAL OFFICERS

Generalmajor (major general).
No star on shoulder strap

Generalleutnant (lieutenant
general). One silver star

General der Infanterie, etc.
(general). Two silver stars

Generaloberst (colonel general).
Three silver stars

Generalfeldmarschall (field marshal). Two crossed batons

chevron (the diamond was not used), a Gefreiter wore the double chevron, and an Obergefreiter wore a triple chevron.

Senior NCOs wore a 9mm band of braiding inside the Waffenfarbe piping on each shoulder strap and progressive ranks were indicated by various combinations of diamond or 'pip', as shown in the accompanying plates. After the outbreak of war in September 1939, the regimental and company numbers shown were removed in most cases, for security reasons. The senior NCO of a unit, whatever his actual rank, also wore a double band of the 9mm wide braiding on each cuff to indicate his status. He was known as 'Der Spiess'. An Oberfeldwebel who was the senior NCO was from September 1938 known as Hauptfeldwebel. A junior NCO who nonetheless, senior NCO of a unit took the tit Acting Hauptfeldwebel.

Company officers had more elaborate shou straps decorated in flat silver braiding backe the Waffenfarbe colour. Field officers had the ver braiding in 'plaited' form, again backed Waffenfarbe. Diamonds or 'pips' were adde indicate the rank differences, as shown in plate. General officers had gold braiding wc each side of a silver strand with the grade i cated by combinations of stars or batons. backing was the bright red of Waffenfarbe general officers.

COLLAR PATCHES

The relation of these to the arm of service colour was described in the section on Waffenfarben. Collar patches relevant to the various ranks are shown in the accompanying plates. However, general officers had their own distinctive collar patches indicating their high rank. From 1942 collar patch for a Generalfeldmarschall lengthened to show one more loop of braid the original style shown in the plate. All braid was in gold woven on a bright red backi

---

DIRECTORS OF MUSIC

Directors of Music (or Bandmasters) who were given ranks equivalent to officers wore more elaborate shoulder straps featuring red and sil- ver-grey (or aluminium) cording, and a device. Stars indicated the grade or rank.

Plate 46: *Directors of Music (Bandmasters).*

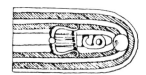

Musikmeister, piped in Waffenfarbe, red and aluminum cords, lyre and numeral gold-colored metal. Band master, junior. Rank of second lieutenant

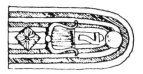

Obermusikmeister, same as Musikmeister, but one gold-colored star, metal. Band master, senior. Rank of first lieutenant

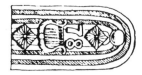

Stabsmusikmeister, same as Obermusikmeister, but two gold-colored metal stars. Chief band master. Rank of captain

te 47: *Officers' quality Hoheitsabzeichen, itioned above right breast pocket.*

te 48: *Officer's collar patch Litzen with ffenfarbe (pink in this case). Note also the metal ton painted field grey and the dark bottle green ing on the collar.*

Plate 49: *Officer's shoulder strap, Oberst (colonel) and divisional or regimental number. Waffenfarbe pink — panzer troops.*

Plate 50: *Service dress tunic for an Oberst showing relative positions of the insignia shown in the previous three plates.*

47

49

50

60

Plate 51: *Officer's shoulder strap, Oberstleutnant (lt-col), no unit number. Waffenfarbe on shoulder strap and collar patch is grass green — motorcycle troops.*

Plate 52: *Prewar pattern pointed shoulder strap with button having company number and printed regimental number (89), but worn on a 1943 pattern tunic with the simplified collar patch and no dark green facing material. Rank: Unteroffizier; Waffenfarbe: black (engineers).*

Plate 53: *Shoulder strap of a private of infantry (Waffenfarbe: white), having slip-on number on field grey strip and single strip of braid indicating a NCO candidate (unteroffizieranwärter). It is on a 1936 pattern tunic.*

Plate 54: *Shoulder straps on a 1936 pattern tunic of a Feldwebel of infantry (Waffenfarbe: white), having a metal regimental number. The dark bottle green facing is omitted from the collar. Note Iron Cross 2nd Class ribbon in second buttonhole.*

Plate 55: *Shoulder straps of Hauptfeldwebel of transport battalion (Waffenfarbe: light blue) showing also the NCO's braid on collar and the dark bottle green facing.*

RANK BADGES FOR CAMOUFLAGE CLOTHING

War conditions led to the introduction of various styles of camouflage and combat clothing for which the conventional types of rank indication evolved for service or tropical dress were not appropriate or desirable. A straightforward and relatively low visibility way of indicating rank by means of simple cloth patches was introduced from August 1942. The badges were worn 10cm below the left shoulder seam. The pattern was derived from a scheme of badges also issued equivalent ranks in the Waffen-SS. The desig were printed in green on black cloth backing f all ranks except general officers who had th designs woven in yellow cotton or black wo The badge for a Generalfeldmarschall incorp rated crossed batons woven in white, in place the three stars shown for a Generaloberst.

Plate 56: *Rank Badges for Camouflage Clothing.*

Stabsfeldwebel

Oberfeldwebel

Feldwebel

Unterfeldwebel

Unteroffizier

Oberstleutnant

Major

Hauptmann

Oberleutnant

Leutnant

Generaloberst

General

Generalleutnant

Generalmajor

Oberst

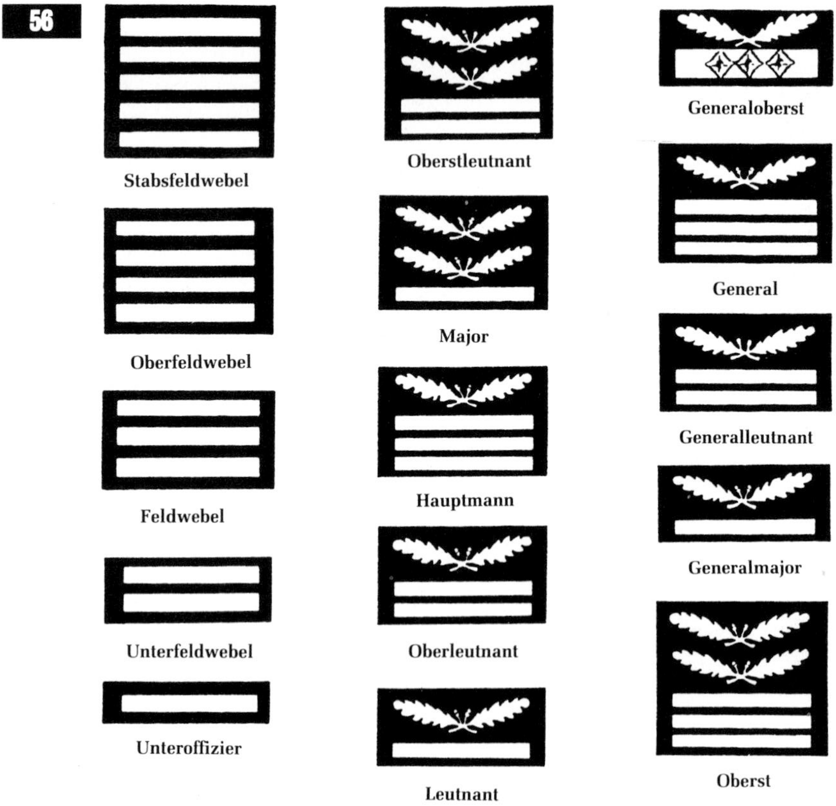

SPECIALIST BADGES

Special skills or functions for which individual enlisted men or NCOs were qualified were indicated by small badges, mostly worn on the lower part of the right sleeve. In most cases the badges were woven in yellow on dark bottle green cloth, but there were some exceptions, noted in th accompanying captions. The captions also not the positions for those badges not worn on th lower right sleeve.

57

 Medical personnel (Sanitätsunterpersonal)

 Fortification maintenance sergeant (Wallmeister)

 Saddler candidate (Truppensattlermeister-Anwärter)

 Pigeoneer (sergeant) (Brieftaubenmeister)

 Paymaster candidate (Anwärter für die Heeres-Zahlmeisterlaufbahn)

 Pyrotechnician (Feuerwerker)

 Motor maintenance sergeant (harness sergeant if horse outfit) (Schirrmeister)

 Fortification construction sergeant (Festungspioneer-Feldwebel)

 Horseshoeing instructor (Hufbeschlaglehrmeister)

 Helmsman (Steuermann). This insignia is worn on the *left upper* sleeve. (Anchor in silver embroidery)

 Horseshoers (personnel) (Hufbeschlagpersonal)

 Operator smoke troops (Bedienungspersonal Nebelabteilung). This insignia is worn on the *left lower* arm. Worked in white rayon on dark green background.

 Radio sergeant (Funkmeister)

 Communication personnel (other than Signal Corps) (Nachrichtenpersonal). This insignia is worn on the *left upper* sleeve. (Flash in "Waffenfarben")

 Army mountain guide (Heeresbergführer). This insignia is worn on the *left breast*

 Ordnance sergeant (Waffenmeister)

 Gunlayer artillery (Richtkanonier). This insignia is worn on *left lower* arm

63

CUFF TITLES

Cuff titles were either printed or woven on to a cloth band for wear around the lower sleeve, commonly 15cm from the lower edge, though there were variations. Cuff titles either indicated specific units or specialisations, though later they were also issued to commemorate momentous actions or theatres of war as a sort of battle honour. Among cuff titles worn by army units were 'Grossdeutschland' (in varying forms) by personnel of this formation; 'Propagandakompanie' by war reporters and photographers within the army; 'Feldpost' by army post office un 'Feldgendarmerie' by all military pol 'Führerhaupquartier' by staff at any of Hitl headquarters; 'Heeresmusikschule' by memb of the army school of music; 'Afrikakorps' members of the Deutsche Afrika Korps; 'Afrika 1943 replacement for the previous one; a 'Kreta' for units involved in the Crete campai There were very many more. Colours varied dark green, black, or brown was common w the lettering in silver or gold.

SPECIAL ARMS BADGES

Some types of unit who were trained in specialist skills had badges to indicate their specialisation. These included the following:

• **Mountain Troops**
Mountain Troops (Gebirgsjäger) formed an important part of the army order of battle in World War 2. Specialising in mountain warfare, they had several items of clothing and equipment peculiar to their needs. From May 1939 a special badge featuring the mountain flower (Edelwei was produced in woven or embroidered form wear on the upper arm. The flower was colou white with yellow threading, with a green st and silver-grey surround. A white metal versi of the same design, but without the surround a canted to the side was worn on the left side of mountain troops' cap.

A further specialist skill badge was worn men qualified as a mountain guide (Bergführe

Plate 58: *Mountain Troops' arm badge.*

Plate 59: *Jäger Troops' arm badge.*

Plate 60: *White metal cap badges for Mountain Troops (left) and Jäger Troops.*

...o featuring the Edelweiss motif. This was an ...amelled badge worn on the left breast pocket ...the service tunic and had a high status value, ...ing only awarded to expert climbers. It pre-...ded the general mountain troops' badge, having ...en introduced in 1936. This badge is illus-...ted in **Plate 47** with the other specialist ...dges.

Jäger Troops

...me elite fighting formations were designated as ...ger troops and they were issued with a woven ...embroidered arm badge of similar size to the ...birgsjäger badge. The design featured green ...k leaves, a brown twig and acorn, and a lighter ...en rope surround. It was instituted late in ...42. Also, like the mountain troops, there was a ...hite metal version of this design, without the ...pe surround, worn on the left side of the forage ...p.

Ski Jäger Troops

...few units, mostly infantry, were specially ...ained as ski troops. They wore a badge very ...milar to the Jäger badge in design, with the ...dition of crossed skis interleaved with the oak ...ves. The corresponding metal cap badge, worn ...the left side, featured the oak leaf design with ...single ski superimposed diagonally.

Feldgendarmerie

...he military police (Feldgendarmerie) had their ...vn distinctive cloth badge worn on the upper ...ft arm and featuring an eagle with swastika ...ith an oak leaf wreath surround. For officers it ...as in silver-grey and for other ranks it was ...ange with a black swastika. On the left cuff was ...orn a cuff title with the word 'Feldgendarmerie' ...ttered in grey gothic script, a grey edging, and a ...own background. On the helmet a transfer ver-

Plate 61: *Feldgendarmerie gorget plate worn by an Unteroffizier.*

sion of the Feldgendarmerie sleeve badge replaced the Wehrmacht eagle transfer on the left side. When on duty men of the Feldgendarmerie worn a metal gorget plate (Ringkraken), lettered 'Feldgendarmerie' and carrying the eagle and swastika badge in embossed form. This plate was slung on a neck chain, positioned just below the collar opening, and was usually painted dull silver-grey. Also occasionally seen was an armband lettered 'Feldgendarmerie' in orange on green, worn on the left arm when on duty by ordinary soldiers seconded to police units. On the gorget

...ate 62: *Feldgendarmerie arm badge and gorget ...ate.*

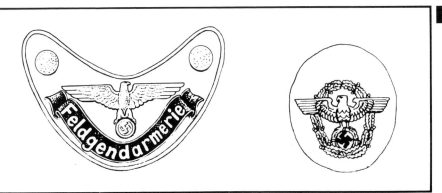

Plate 63: *Bandsmen wearing 'Swallow's Nest' wings.*

Plate 65: *A private (Schütze) on sentry duty in Oslo, April 1940, showing the basic 1936 pattern service dress. Note side sling on the 98K rifle and the ammunition pouches on the belt. The equipment braces are not being worn.*

Plate 64: *Bandsman wearing 'Swallow's Nest' wings with the black special tank troops' uniform. Note regimental number (3) on sewn-down shoulder strap.*

Plate 66: *Service tunic, 1936 pattern, without the da green facing material on the collar. The rank denote is Feldwebel.*

plate, the end rivets, eagle emblem, and embossed lettering, were finished in luminous paint.

• **Musicians and Bandsmen**
Military band personnel when on duty wore the traditional 'Swallow's Nest' 'wings' on the shoulder (Schwalbennester). These varied according to qualification. Men of the drum and fife corps had strips of dull grey braid over a Waffenfarbe backing (eg, white for an infantry battalion) in the appropriate colour. Men of the regimental band had silver-coloured braid on a Waffenfarbe back-

ing in the appropriate colour (eg, pink for an armoured regiment). Battalion buglers had the same type as the bandsmen with the addition of a lace fringe 7cm long. These wings were attached by hooks to eyelets worked into the man's shoulder seams on service and uniform tunics. Thus the wings could be worn with the special uniforms issued to tank crews in the case of armoured regiments' musicians, though they are more commonly associated with ordinary service and parade dress. They were not worn with greatcoats.

1936-PATTERN SERVICE DRESS

In 1933 when Hitler came to power, the men of the Reichsheer were wearing a service dress uniform introduced in the early 1920s to replace the 1915 pattern uniform introduced for the Imperial Army in general wear at the time of the Armistice. However, an improved design of the Reichsheer uniform in hand was intended to update the cut and style to make it more comfortable. Prototypes were tested in the field in 1934 and it was adopted and quickly issued in 1936 as the 1936 pattern service dress (Heeres Dienstanzug).

The tunic (Feldbluse) was of field grey wool material with a turn-down collar. The front buttoned to the neck and had five field grey metal buttons. A neckband, removable for washing, was fitted with small collar studs inside the tunic collar. In the field it was permitted to wear the tunic with the top button undone. There were four patch pockets, each with box pleats and secured with three-pointed flaps and field grey metal buttons. The pockets were arranged one on each breast and one in each front skirt. There was a concealed inside pocket in the righthand skirt, 17cm wide and 18cm deep and secured by a button. When on active service a standard field dressing pack was carried in this pocket. There was a single vent 15cm deep in the lower back and the jacket was shaped at the waist. Around the waist were four metal supports to which the waistbelt fitted. These fitted in eyelet holes which were positioned vertically in groups of three to give some variation in the exact position of the waistbelt depending on the wearer's physique and wishes. The collar was faced with dark bottle green material. Detachable shoulder straps, secured by a button, were fitted to the tunic and were also faced in dark bottle green material in the case of other ranks, but with the various rank and unit distinctions previously described. Until 1938 these shoulder straps had blunt pointed ends for other ranks, but the shape was then changed to a rounded end. Both types could be seen in use, and the earlier pattern

shoulder strap was still in wear by some units or individuals well into the war period. The sleeve cuffs were plain with a split at the back to allow the cuffs to be drawn together and buttoned in cold weather.

Officers' service dress tunics were nominally of the same cut and style as the men's, except that the sleeve cuffs had a turn-back rather than plain ends. Better quality material was normally used as the tunics were privately tailored. However, it was not uncommon, particularly in the later war years, for officers to use the ordinary issue service tunic as issued to other ranks, except that it was, of course, fitted with officers' shoulder straps and officers' quality breast badge and collar patches. Conversely some senior NCOs were occasionally seen with privately tailored tunics of officers' quality. While the standard issue service tunic was of excellent quality and good material (originally 80% wool, 20% rayon), the quality declined from quite early in the war as economies were made and demands for supply increased. Pictorial evidence suggests that as early as mid-1941 tunics were being issued with plain collars and shoulder straps, the dark bottle green material being omitted.

The matching trousers for the 1936 pattern service tunic were also made from field grey wool material. When first standardised in 1936 the trousers were made in a shade of bluish grey, but it was later realised that this would complicate production, because of differing dye requirements, and in 1939 field grey became the standard colour for trousers. The trousers had side split pockets, a four-button fly front, and a high waist with a higher 'V' cut into the back. Suspenders (braces) held the trousers up but there was a small buckle strap at the rear to tighten the fit at the waist. The trousers had straight legs and could be worn with high boots, ankle boots and gaiters, or shoes/boots only when walking out. Because tunics and trousers were not all made together, there was often some shade variation

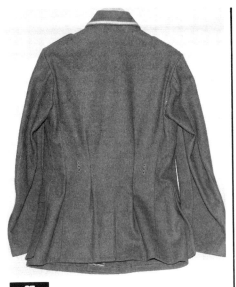

67

68

Plate 67: *Rear view of 1936 pattern service tunic, showing 15cm central vent.*

Plate 68: *Service tunic, 1936 pattern, with dark green facing material on collar. Rank of Hauptfeldwebel with twin braid cuff rings of unit senior NCO, 'Der Spiess'.*

Plate 69: *Close view of 1936 pattern tunic showing pocket pleats, metal buttons painted field grey, triple eyelets at waist for belt support clips and sewn-in loops on breast to affix decorations. Twin 9mm braid cuff bands of 'Der Spiess'.*

Plate 70: *The 1936 service dress in field wear. Top right and bottom left tunics lack the dark bottle green facing; the other two have it. The Unteroffizier (centre) wears the Knight's Cross, Iron Cross 1st Class and the infantry assault badge. He has a standard Wehrmacht flashlight hanging from his second tunic button and a Luger pistol holster. His Feldmütze is carried in his belt. Note leather braces pass under the shoulder straps and all other straps go over them. The private behind to the left wears his haversack but no braces, and has the anti-gas cape valise on his chest, all in brown leather.*

which could be accentuated with age, wear and fading.

Mounted troops (cavalry, horse transport, etc) wore field grey riding breeches as an alternative to trousers. Officers could also wear riding breeches, of superior material when tailor-made. Riding breeches were quite commonly seen in wear by officers on staff or administrative duties.

The shirt issued to other ranks (but also worn by officers) to wear beneath the tunic was mouse grey in colour in its basic form, with long sleeves, long tails and a fixed collar with a buttoned chest. It did not button right down the front, however, so had to be pulled on or off over the head. This shirt was in wool material, quite thick. It replaced an earlier pre-war shirt of similar cut which was white in colour and was issued until 1939. When hostilities commenced it was realised that this was too conspicuous when the tunic was removed, hence its replacement by a grey version. When the tunic was worn and fully buttoned-up the shirt was not, of course, visible.

Plate 71: *Officer's 1936 pattern service tunic, showing turn-back cuffs and superior quality material.*

Plate 72: *Sorting mail on the Russian Front, summer 1942: three of the men here are wearing the grey wool issue shirt, but the man nearest left is wearing a check pattern civilian shirt. He is also wearing gaiters. Also shown, right, is the waist shape of the service dress trousers.*

A second pattern shirt was issued which was more practical for hot weather when the tunic might be discarded to allow 'shirt-sleeve order'. This improved shirt was field grey in colour, had attachments on the shoulder to allow the shoulder straps to be affixed from the tunic, and it had two buttoned patch pockets on the breast. Shirt collars were normally worn open. In the closing stages of the war an order was made allowing officers to wear a tie with the shirt and turn back the tunic revers to reveal it. Pictorial evidence suggests that non-standard civilian shirts were sometimes worn under the service dress tunic. On campaign a non-regulation neck scarf could also be seen, worn round the shirt collar when the top buttons of the tunic were left undone.

Officers, specifically, often wore white shirts underneath their tunics.

Footwear

The footwear most associated with the German Army of almost any modern period is the marching boot (Marschstiefel), commonly called a 'jackboot'. It was the most widely issued item of footwear through most of the Third Reich era and was made of black leather. Also issued was a black leather ankle boot (Schnürschuhe) which was also commonly seen in wear. From 1943 onwards the ankle boot became increasingly common, worn with gaiters, as leather supplies were reduced with a consequent effect on marching boot supplies. However, in appropriate circumstances the combination of ankle boots and gaiters could be seen in wear throughout the war period. The gaiters were made of field grey or sage green canvas with leather edging and straps. Some earlier, taller, leather gaiters from the Reichsheer era could also be seen on occasion, particularly in secondary units, in the earlier part

of the war, and in the prewar period. Also issued for wear with ankle boots were canvas puttees of the wrap-around sort, made in thick field grey cloth (Wickelgamaschen). For 'walking out' and informal occasions, plain black privately purchased leather shoes could also be worn.

For wear with riding breeches, by officers and personnel of mounted units, there were standard black leather riding boots which had an adjustable buckled top and could be fitted with spurs. There was also a superior quality black leather riding boot, lacking the buckled strap, for wear by officers, but a variety of non-standard riding boost, sometimes in brown leather, were also to be seen as a result of private purchase. Finally there was a lightweight black shoe issued for sports use. All these types of footwear could be seen worn with service dress, though other footwear for specialised or tropical use was issued and will be described in the appropriate sections.

Headwear

Worn with service dress on parade or formal occasions was the service peaked cap (Schirmmütze). This was a conventional forage cap of service type with gloss black peak, dark bottle green hatband, and field grey crown with a wire stiffener inside. Around the edge of the crown and above and below the band, was piping in the appropriate Waffenfarbe. For other ranks there was a black gloss leather chinstrap secured by

74

Plate 74: *Infantry wearing ankle boots and gaiters are pictured in Russia during 1942. All three Unteroffiziers leading this platoon have the infantry assault badge, two have the Iron Cross 1st Class and one (on the right) has the Iron Cross 2nd Class, wearing the ribbon only.*

Plate 75: *New recruits in 1943 wearing ankle boots and puttees on basic training. Their instructors, at left, wear marching boots. The instructor (second from left, front row) is a NCO candidate with single braid strip on his shoulder strap.*

gloss black buttons and normally strapped tight above the peak (though it could, of course be loosened and worn under the chin). The Reich-kokarde and national emblem with oakleaf sur-ound, as previously described, was worn on the front of the cap. Officers wore the same style of cap but with silver cord chinstrap and silver-coloured buttons. Privately-made caps had superior quality cloth and finish. Officer candidates were also allowed to wear this type of cap as were the most senior NCOs. Generals wore the same pattern cap but with the chinstrap cords in gold-braided material secured with gilt buttons. The piping for all generals was in gold-coloured cord rather than in Waffenfarbe.

The only further variation was for Army Chaplains and Bishops who had an officers' quality cap with a small cross set between the national emblem and the Reichskokarde on the front. The Waffenfarbe piping was violet for a chaplain and gold for a bishop.

Plate 76: *Officer's peaked cap (Schirmmütze). Waffenfarbe: grass green — motorcycle troops.*

71

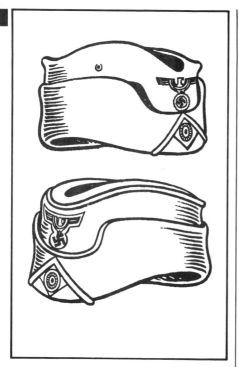

Plate 77: *Feldmütze, 1938 pattern.*

Plate 78: *Einheitsfeldmütze, 1943 pattern (left) and officer's old-style field cap showing soft leather peak and no cords.*

For wear on campaign or on less formal occasions, all ranks were issued with a field cap (Feldmütze). The 1938 pattern Feldmütze, issued prewar, was made in lined field grey cloth and was of the type sometimes called a 'garrison cap' or 'field service cap' in other armies. It was of fore-and-aft type with folded side flaps which could be let down in inclement weather to cover the ears and fit under the chin. The folded-up front of the Feldmütze carried an inverted chevron in Waffenfarbe colour with a cloth Reichskokarde inside the apex of this. The national emblem was carried above, on the front of the crown. The officers' version of this same cap varied by having silver-grey piping around the crown and around the front turn-up. It was also, usually, of superior quality material. The version for generals had gilt piping and decoration instead of silver.

With the wartime economies, a new version of the Feldmütze was issued from July 1942. The 1942 pattern Feldmütze differed from the 1938 pattern in having the fold-down section secured at the front by two small metal buttons, painted field grey, which allowed the lower part of the cap to be folded down over the ears with the buttons then used to secure the front flaps below the chin. On the front of the cap the badge was reduced to the national emblem and Reichskokarde embroidered on an inverted cloth triangle. There was no Waffenfarbe. This cap was simpler to manufacture than the 1938 pattern version but it was, in fact, a simplified version of the earlier Reichsheer Feldmütze which the 1938 pattern cap had replaced. The 1938 pattern cap remained in use, of course, with those issued **with them before the 1942 pattern appeared.**

7

Plate 79: *The 1943 Einheitsfeldmütze and possible method of wearing it in cold weather.*

Plate 80: *1942 pattern Feldmütze.*

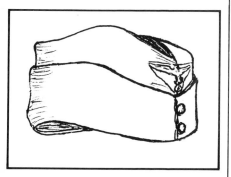

Both these types of field cap could be worn under the steel helmet.

Instead of the Feldmütze those officers who had them often preferred to wear the original style of officer's field cap, the Offizierfeldmütze, which dated from the 1930s. This was a simplified version of the peaked cap, Schirmmütze, lacking the wire stiffener and the chinstrap cords. It had a softer peak and cloth embroidered badges rather than white metal versions. Because it lacked a stiffener, this cap tended to be fashioned into various 'battered' shapes, but it is important to note that in the field the Schirmmütze was also to be seen worn by officers with the stiffener removed so that the crown again assumed a 'battered' shape. The officer's field cap was officially declared obsolete in April 1942, but was so popular that it was to be seen in use until the end of the war.

Designed to supplement or replace all the previous types of field cap was the 1943 pattern Standard Field Cap (Einheitsfeldmütze). This was a field grey soft cap with a close fitting crown and fold-down side-flaps, plus a long cloth peak.

It was derived from the designs of field cap used by the Afrika Korps and Mountain Troops (described later) and was of a shape sometimes called a 'ski cap'. The fold-down flaps were secured in front by two small field grey metal buttons, and could be secured under the chin when the side-flaps were folded down over the ears. On the front of the crown was worn an embroidered (later sometimes printed) combination of the national emblem and Reichskokarde on an inverted field grey cloth triangle. The officer's version of the cap had silver-grey piping around the edge of the crown and the general's version had gilt piping around the crown. This cap was introduced in June 1943 and rapidly came into almost universal use. In the later months of the war it could even be seen in wear at formal parades and occasions in place of the old service peaked cap.

Steel Helmets

The German steel helmet (Stahlhelm) with its 'coal scuttle' shape is probably the most easily recognised item of German military uniform. The original type in use was introduced in World War 1 as the 1916 pattern helmet. It was used by the Reichsheer and the Heer, virtually unchanged. A distinctive feature was the small lug on each side originally intended to take a pivoted face visor for use by snipers. However, this helmet was heavy and a lighter more abbreviated version to the same shape, but slightly shallower, was designed called the 1935 pattern helmet based on a prototype design which had been troop trialled in 1934. The new 1935 pattern helmet was issued starting in 1936 and rapidly replaced the 1916 pattern helmet. However, some units were still to be seen with the 1916 pattern helmet in the early part of the war and the early pattern remained in issue with the second-line or training units and others throughout the war. A slightly simplified helmet (the 1943 pattern) was introduced in 1943, being a one-piece pressing without the neat edging found on the 1935 pattern helmet. Still to be seen occasionally in the 1930s was the 1918

Plate 81: *The 1916 pattern helmet (left) compared directly with the smaller, lighter 1935 pattern. Note the Wehrmacht eagle transfer.*

pattern cavalry helmet which resembled the 1916 pattern helmet in shape but had distinctive 'scallop' shapes in the rim on each side.

German steel helmets were painted field grey inside and out and had a padded sprung leather inner lining which was slightly adjustable, plus a black leather chinstrap, adjustable for fit, and detachable. Various covers and fittings for camouflage purposes could be seen on the helmet under campaign conditions. These included coloured cloth bands for exercise purposes (to identify 'opposing' forces); leather or rubber bands to hold local foliage; net crown to hold local foliage; overall net cover to hold local foliage; and cloth covers in various colours — white, sand, sage green and drab pattern. Cloth covers sometimes had loops worked into them to take local foliage. Paint, mud or sand thrown on wet paint, were also used to camouflage helmets.

Plate 82: *1935 pattern steel helmet with the field grey overpainted in sand colour for the Afrika Korps. Right, officer's peaked cap with the stiffener removed allowing it to be worn in a 'soft' shape in the field. Waffenfarbe on this example is pink, indicating panzer troops.*

Design of a new simplified helmet was undertaken in 1944, the object being to produce a lighter, cheaper item that gave comparable protection to the earlier patterns. Though some pre-production helmets to the new design were tested in the last six months of the war, no production took place. However, the new design, with a deeper rear edge, was revived for the East German Nationalvolksarmee (NVA) in the postwar German Democratic Republic, and was commonly seen prior to the disbandment of the NVA in 1991.

Personal Equipment

Personal equipment was based on a belt-and-brace set to which further items could be added depending on the wearer's unit or duty. Enlisted men who carried a rifle had a 1909 pattern ammunition pouch on the belt each side of the buckle. This pouch was divided into three sections, each holding 10 rounds in clips. The belt passed through loops at the back of each pouch. The centre section of each pouch had a D-ring to which the leather equipment braces, when worn, could be hooked. The belt also carried the entrenching tool in a leather frog on the left. Originally the bayonet was carried over the entrenching tool from a leather loop on the entrenching tool frog, However, it was moved forward of the entrenching tool early in the war, to hang separately in its own leather frog. A 1934 pattern haversack (Brotbeutel-bread bag) in brown canvas was suspended from two loops behind the right hip. It held the Feldmütze (when not being worn), toiletries, eating utensils and rations. A D-ring on the Brotbeutel, with a retaining strap, carried the 1931 pattern aluminium water bottle. The leather equipment braces passed over each shoulder and secured to the belt at the back. D-rings were fitted to each brace behind the shoulder and these were used to suspend a light metal, web-covered yoke. From this yoke could be suspended the assault pack haversack or a full marching order pack, the Tornister, which was of fur-covered hide. In either of these orders the greatcoat, blanket and Zeltbahn were rolled and carried in a 'horseshoe' over the top of the pack. However, whenever possible the back packs were carried in unit transport and were most often seen in wear when a unit was entraining or on the move between bases. The anti-gas respirator in a ribbed cylindrical case was carried on a separate web strap over the right shoulder and could be hooked at the bottom onto the belt at the rear. A poncho or anti-gas cape could be suspended from the waist belt, but could also be carried in a pouch with strap over the chest for immediate use. When the threat of gas did not materialise, this item was less often seen.

Appropriate pouches for the MP38/MP40 submachine gun ammunition boxes (or other weapons) could replace the rifle ammunition

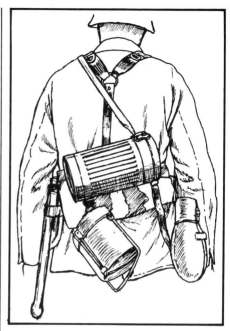

Plate 83: *Personal equipment from the rear showing the anti-gas respirator case hooked at the bottom to the belt, the camouflaged shelter, bread bag, water bottle, canteen, and entrenching tool all suspended from the waistbelt. Note D-ring positions at shoulder.*

Plate 84: *MP38/MP40 magazine pouches attached to braces.*

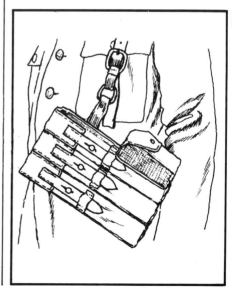

Plate 85: *The personal equipment being worn outside the later (simpler) pattern greatcoat, with the camouflage shelter and blanket rolled and carried on top of the haversack. Note also the bayonet carried separately in its own frog in later style, and cord to support foliage on the helmet.*

Plate 86: *Infantry in Russia in 1944 wearing full marching order with the camouflage shelter and blanket rolled together and 'horseshoed' over the Tornister pack, though the leading man is simply carrying a bundle of gear. Note the rifle slung in front, the later (simpler) pattern of greatcoat, and the Einheitsfeldmütze.*

Plate 87: *An infantry Gefrieter in full marching order with the fur-covered Tornister pack, rolled camouflage shelter, a full-size spade in the entrenching tool frog, and a field telephone set carried on the belt front — he is probably a regimental signaller. The general carrying out the inspection carries his baton and wears the old Reichsheer pattern service tunic with sloped diagonal lower pockets. He wears light grey kid gloves and is a Knight's Cross holder. The general (centre background) wears the old pattern officer's field cap and a 1936 pattern service tunic. The date is spring 1940.*

Plate 88: *Two soldiers in greatcoats pictured on the Russian Front, late in 1941. They wear the standard greatcoat with waistbelt from the personal equipment. Note stick grenade carried in belt. The nearest man wears the standard field grey leather gloves with ribbed backs, and the furthest man wears knitted dark grey gloves and also has a helmet band for the affixing of camouflage foliage.*

Plate 89: *Assault engineers practice river crossing in Kleine Flossack rubber boats in January 1941. They are wearing full equipment with the assault pack haversack on the back and greatcoat/blanket roll 'horseshoed' over it. Note rifles slung to the front.*

Plate 90: *Very typical variation in wear of personal equipment is seen on these three soldiers on the Russian Front in the summer of 1942. The nearest man wears canteen, bread bag, entrenching tool nearest to the 'regulation' positions.*

Plate 91: *The inferior cut and quality of the 1943 pattern service tunic is evident in this view which shows 'wrinkling' in the arms. Note the lack of pleats on the pockets. It is fitted with prewar style pointed shoulder straps.*

pouches, or a holster for a pistol could be worn on the waist belt as required. All side arms carried slings to enable them to be slung from the shoulders or carried across the front of the body. Belt, braces etc, were all in black leather, with D-rings and other fittings in gunmetal. The belt had a distinctive white metal buckle carrying the motto 'Gott Mit Uns' (God with us). Junior officers under combat conditions could be seen wearing all or part of the belt-and-braces set, particularly when carrying side arms. The actual belt for officers, however, was in brown leather with a conventional open frame buckle. Until the outbreak of war, officers also wore a brown leather cross-belt of 'Sam Browne' type, but this was discontinued as it made the officers too easy to spot by enemy sharpshooters.

Greatcoats

A greatcoat was issued for wear over service dress, this being made of field grey wool material with a deep fold-down collar, which could be turned up and buttoned with a flap at the front for cold weather wear. The collar was faced with dark bottle green material and shoulder straps of detachable kind (same as for the tunic) were worn appropriate to rank and status. the greatcoat was nominally the same pattern for all ranks below general. It had deep turn-back cuffs, a half-

belt and two buttons at the back, and full pleated skirts reaching below the knee. On parades and formal occasions the service belt was worn outside the greatcoat. On campaign the full personal equipment set was also worn over the greatcoat. Officers could be seen wearing standard issue greatcoats, but very often they had them made privately by military tailors in a superior quality material similar to their service dress. Officers of general rank also had the standard pattern great coat but it had gilt buttons instead of field grey and the inside of the front flaps had bright red facings. The top two buttons were left undone and the lapels showed the red facings to the front.

As an alternative to the greatcoat, officers were allowed to wear a field grey leather overcoat which was supplied by military tailors. This was cut in a similar style to the greatcoat but there were variations in detail. Shoulder straps were supposed to be worn with this coat but were sometimes omitted. There were some minor variation in greatcoat style. The most notable was a later version which omitted the dark bottle green facing material and left the collar in plain field grey. In addition some coats were locally modified by wearers, especially on the Russian front for example to fit fur collars.

As the war lengthened and Germany's resources were stretched, numerous economies were effected. In the case of uniforms a major change was the simplification of service dress garments. The tunic (Feldbluse) was changed to have slightly shorter skirts and plain pockets (no pleats) with shorter straight edged flaps. All the dark bottle green facing material was omitted and the collar Litzen was reduced to a very inferior embroidered type. The material used was of much lower quality with a definite 'shoddy' look and feel about it. The wool content was much reduced and recycled wool was usually used, together with a greater percentage of artificial fibres. The resulting garment was less hard wearing than the earlier patterns and looked less smart. It should be emphasised that the 1936 pattern tunic remained on issue (while stocks lasted) and refurbished tunics were re-issued, and this earlier tunic was also to be seen without the dark bottle green facing material. Thus in the last two years of the war there was a mix of both types of tunic to be seen.

The service trousers were similarly reduced in quality, but a saving in material was also made by reducing the waist shape to ordinary self-supporting type with attached belt, and dispensing with provision for suspenders (braces).

The greatcoat was similarly changed. It lost all its dark bottle green facing material and became less elegant in shape owing to the inferior material. The 1943 pattern greatcoat, however, had a distinctive deep collar which could give better protection in inclement weather, when turned up. Variations on this coat existed, including one with a pair of extra slit side pockets above the normal side pockets, and added lining especially for winter combat wear.

The 1943 pattern Standard Field Cap (Einheitsfeldmütze) already described was strictly speaking part of the 1943 service dress revisions.

Plate 92: *The Obergefreiter here, being congratulated on his wedding, wears the skimpier 1943 pattern service tunic. Note the absence of facing material on the collar. The officer wears the old-style officer's service cap and the old Reichsheer pattern service tunic. The officer at extreme left wears brown kid gloves.*

Plate 93: *Details of personal equipment and associated items carried by the combat soldier (drawings by Shin Ueda, Tamiya Co).*

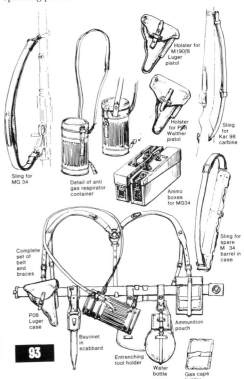

Holster for M190/8 Luger pistol

Holster for P38 Walther pistol

Sling for Kar 98 carbine

Sling for MG 34

Detail of anti gas respirator container

Ammo boxes for MG34

Sling for spare M 34 barrel in case

Complete set of belt and braces

P08 Luger case

Bayonet in scabbard

Ammunition pouch

Entrenching tool holder

Water bottle

Gas cape holder

93

Chevron indicates a Gefreiter (lance-corporal) and the shield is a campaign badge for the Crimea

MG 34. gunner wearing 1936 pattern tunic with no facing material on collar or shoulder straps; note that a rifleman would wear another ammunition pouch instead of the P08 holster

Note hooks to support belt

Pattern 1936 tunic showing pleated pockets and facings in dark bottle green

Pattern 1943 tunic with plain pockets, no facing material on collar and shoulder straps

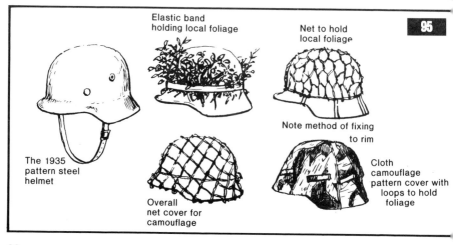

Elastic band holding local foliage

Net to hold local foliage

Note method of fixing to rim

The 1935 pattern steel helmet

Overall net cover for camouflage

Cloth camouflage pattern cover with loops to hold foliage

Plate 94: *Direct comparison between the 1936 and 1943 pattern service tunics showing details (drawings by Shin Ueda, Tamiya Co).*

Plate 95: *Typical helmet variations (drawings by Shin Ueda, Tamiya Co).*

Plate 96: *A soldier receives an award, wearing the camouflage helmet cover and 1943 pattern service tunic which does, however, seem to have dark green collar facing and the older-pattern collar patches.*

Plate 97: *The anti-gas respirator in wear, and the straps affixed to the helmet to hold local foliage in place.*

Plate 98: *Assault engineers cross the River Meuse on the opening day of the French campaign in May 1940. Local foliage has been attached to the helmet bands.*

To effect further economies a new type of service dress, based closely on British battledress, was introduced in September 1944. This consisted of a field grey tunic (Feldbluse) in blouse form with a 12cm waistband and no skirts. It had two non-pleated breast pockets with plain button-down flaps. The six-button front allowed the top button to be left undone and the collar worn open and turned back. Badges and insignia were of the simplified type, printed or embroidered. Supports for personal equipment could be fitted to the waistband of the blouse, but only one eyehole was fitted for the support clips instead of three vertical holes, giving a choice of height, as on previous tunics. The later self-supporting trousers, ankle boots and gaiters, and the 1943 pattern Einheitsfeldmütze were invariably worn with the 1944 pattern blouse. The older type of shoulder strap could be seen attached to this blouse, but the later plain field grey type was more common. The cuffs of the blouse were similar in style to previous tunics and could be buttoned tight if required. Some officers had tailored versions of the 1944 pattern tunic with variations such as pointed pocket flaps and fly fronts concealing the buttons. Generals carried their distinctive red/braid collar patches in place of the usual Litzen collar patches. The 1944 pattern issue was still not in widespread wear when the war ended.

99

100

82

Plate 99: *The 1944 pattern service dress, showing the simplified field blouse similar to British battledress blouse.*

Plate 100: *Three different examples of the late war-pattern Bevo-type national emblem in 'utility' style. The black example (right) is for the black panzer troops' blouse. The small version is for the field cap. Though they could be cut to triangular shape before stitching in place, the correct procedure was to fold the backing to triangular shape before stitching.*

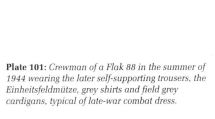

Plate 101: *Crewman of a Flak 88 in the summer of 1944 wearing the later self-supporting trousers, the Einheitsfeldmütze, grey shirts and field grey cardigans, typical of late-war combat dress.*

MOUNTAIN TROOPS

Mountain troops (Gebirgsjäger) wore a version of the standard service dress adapted for their special duties. The Feldbluse was of the ordinary service type with appropriate shoulder straps and insignia according to rank and status, and the Edelweiss sleeve badge was worn. The service trousers were gathered in at the ankle and worn with high-cut mountain climbing boots. Some variations on this were common, especially in the 1939-40 period. Officers, in particular, often favoured wrap-around field grey cloth puttees or civilian-style spats. Tyrolean-type wool stockings, reaching nearly to the knees outside thick climbing breeches were, in fact, the prewar style for mountain troops and they continued in wear with some units in the early part of the war. Staff officers could be seen in breeches and riding boots as a further variation in dress, while the ordinary service marching boot could also be seen in wear by mountain troops on occasion.

The headwear for mountain troops was a distinctive peaked Mountain Cap (Gebirgsmütze); this carried a white metal Edelweiss badge on the left side of the cap. The Gebirgsmütze was derived from the Austrian Army forage cap which had been in use for many years. The 1943

Plate 102: *A typical man of the Mountain Troops wearing the army pattern camouflage smock, white side outwards. Note also the mountain cap, puttees and climbing boots.*

Plate 103: *Sage green wind jacket, issued to about 10% of all mountain troops.*

Plate 104: *The 1943 pattern windproof suit for mountain troops was reversible, one side white and other side tan in colour. Note three pockets across the front.*

Plate 105: *A mountain troops' mule handler wearing the rucksack and personal equipment. Note puttees and climbing boots. This dates from 1938 before the Edelweiss arm badge was issued.*

84

pattern Einheitsfeldmütze was in turn derived from the Gebirgsmütze but had a longer peak. A white cover for the Gebirgsmütze was issued for use in winter snow conditions. The standard steel helmet was also issued to mountain troops, of course.

A distinctive garment issued to mountain troops in the early part of the war was a sage green waterproof wind jacket, double-breasted and reaching to the thighs. This coat was issued to only about 10% of the men and it was supplemented and largely replaced from 1939 by a windproof anorak with drawstring neck and two breast pockets. It was reversible, being field grey on one side and white on the other, and it had an attached hood.

In 1943 a new pattern windproof rayon suit was issued consisting of a reversible anorak and trouser overalls in the same proofed material. Both garments were white on one side and tan on the other. The anorak had a hood, a drawstring waist, and three pockets each (each side) across the chest. The standard reversible camouflage smock (described later) was also issued to mountain troops and, conversely, the 1943 pattern anorak described above was also issued to some other troops operating in mountain areas, as found in the Italian campaign.

Ski trousers and ski boots were also worn in appropriate circumstances and were issued to all mountain troops. Also favoured by mountain troops were Bergen-style rucksacks in place of the normal issue of personal equipment, though this was, of course, widely used by mountain troops.

In general, Ski Jäger companies were also issued with specialist mountain troops' clothing and equipment.

Plate 106: *A mountain troops' gun battery in action. Note the gunlayer on the left in the wind jacket, with cap reversed to facilitate looking through the gunsight.*

Plate 107: *Mountain troops' Gebirgsführer (mountain leader) in standard service dress, with climbing boots and wearing the mountain leader breast badge.*

Plate 108: *Mountain troops in (left to right) wind jacket, cold weather animal skin coat and straw-filled cold weather boots, and ordinary service dress.*

For duty in tanks and armoured cars, a special black service uniform (Sonderbekleidung) was issued. This consisted of a short double-breasted tunic (or blouse), and trousers which were gathered in at the ankle and worn with leather ankle boots. The tunic had a turned-down collar and deep revers which were opened to reveal the standard issue grey shirt with attached collar, with which a black wool tie was worn. The tunic front could be buttoned up to the neck, however, if required. Distinctive 'Death's Head' (skull) devices in white metal were worn within piped patches on the collar to continue the old German cavalry 'Death's Head Hussar' tradition. The shoulder straps were black and showed rank distinctions in the usual way. The dark bottle green facing material was not used. The shoulder straps were sewn in place on the blouse, and buttons were concealed by a fly front, the object being to reduce the risk of any item of clothing catching on projections inside a tank. The black colour is thought to have been inspired by the British tank crew overalls which were also originally black, chosen to conceal the oil stains and dirt from inside early tanks. The national emblem on the right breast was in white or light grey cotton embroidery on a black backing for other ranks, silver thread for NCOs, and silver wire for officers, but there was some variation. The arm of service colour (Waffenfarbe) was carried round the edge of the collar and the collar patches as well as the shoulder straps. In the case of Panzer troops this colour was rose pink, but there was an exception in the 24 Panzer-Division which wore the yellow cavalry Waffenfarbe as it had been converted from 1 Kavallerie-Division. From May 1940 Panzer Pioneer Company personnel also wore the special black uniform and their Waffenfarbe was a twist of black/white. During 1942 the amount of Waffenfarbe was greatly reduced when it was discontinued round the edge of the collar. The various distinctions and insignia specified for ordinary service dress were worn in corresponding positions on the special black uniform.

A special form of headwear was designed for tank troops, protective in nature. This was the Schutzmütze, a floppy black beret worn over a leather dome-like crash helmet. The beret completely concealed the helmet itself. The beret carried the national emblem above the Reichskokarde in woven silver or silver-grey thread. This particular form of headwear was discontinued in early 1940 and was replaced with a black version of the 1938 pattern Feldmütze. In turn this was replaced from 1943 by a black version of the 1943 pattern Einheitsfeldmütze. Both the 1938 pattern Feldmütze and the 1943 pattern Einheitsfeldmütze could be seen in wear in the last two years of the war. The field grey versions of these caps were occasionally seen with the special black uniform though officially only the black caps were to be worn with the black uniform. Officers were sometimes seen wearing the old style peaked service cap with the black uniform, and the standard steel helmet could also be seen in wear. Various other combinations of clothing could be seen at times. It was possible to see men in the field grey service dress but with one or other of the black caps since service dress was issued in any case. Originally the special black uniform was intended to be worn only on duty in tanks, but the uniform was so popular that armour personnel took to wearing it all the time instead of the service dress, even for parades and walking out. Armoured unit bandsmen could similarly be seen in the special black uniform with the 'Swallow's Nest' wings attached. There was no matching black greatcoat so the field grey greatcoat was worn over the black uniform. Yet further non-standard combinations of dress could include field grey service trousers and marching boots with the black **blouse, or camouflage smocks worn with the**

Plate 109: *The special black service dress for tank crews — a close view of the jacket.*

Plate 110: *Detail view of the collar, shoulder straps and insignia, for the rank of leutnant.*

Plate 111: *Detail of the black jacket insignia and the Schutzmütze helmet.*

Plate 112: *The special black uniform in wear in 1940.*

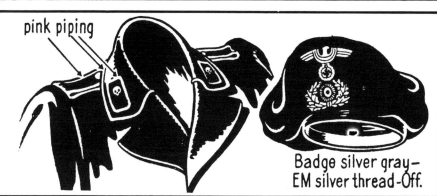

pink piping

Badge silver gray—
EM silver thread-Off.

black trousers, service dress tunics worn with the black trousers, and so on.

In 1940 when the first assault guns were put into service, a new uniform was designed for the crews of these vehicles. This was a field grey version of the special black service uniform described above. It was similar in all respects except that the Schutzmütze was not worn — it had been discontinued before the first assault guns entered service. Any appropriate headgear — helmet, service cap, Feldmütze, etc — could be seen worn with this uniform. Field grey was chosen instead of black for this uniform since many assault guns were open-topped and field grey was a less conspicuous colour in the field than black. Originally the collar patch on the special field grey uniform was the same as that on the black uniform, a 'Death's Head' badge on a black patch with Waffenfarbe surround. However, these were soon replaced by ordinary Litzen patches as worn on the standard service dress tunic. Generals in the special field grey uniform wore their distinctive red collar patches as with ordinary service dress.

Marching boots, ankle boots, or ankle boots and gaiters could be worn with the special field grey service dress, as could the various forms of head dress. Bandsmen in assault gun units could also wear the 'Swallow's Nest' wings on this uniform. Also possible were the various combinations of smock and blouse noted for the black uniform.

In addition to the wool-based special service dress in black and field grey described above, a dress in identical style and cut but made in reed green denim material was issued from 1942. This was a lightweight combination intended for summer use, but sometimes worn at other times. Occasionally the blouse or trousers from this denim suit were worn with the wool equivalent from the special uniform. Thus it was possible for the black blouse to be worn with the reed green trousers, and so on. On some examples of the denim suit, a large patch pocket was included on the breast to hold a map.

Plate 113: A tank regiment commander in the special black uniform in 1942, wearing the black version of the 1938 pattern Feldmütze. His rank is Oberst (colonel).

Plate 114: A tank regiment Feldwebel in 1943, wearing the black version of the Einheitsfeldmütze.

Plate 115: Tank crews after combat on the Russian Front, showing both the special black uniform and the reed green lightweight version of it (centre three). Just visible on the man at second left is his identity disc hanging round his neck (more usually inside the shirt).

Plate 116: The field grey version of the special uniform for tank crews was also worn by assault gun crews. The commander of this StuG III in 1944 wears the Einheitsfeldfmütze and the standard pattern collar patches.

113

Tropical clothing first made its appearance in early 1941 when the advance units of what became the Afrika Korps arrived in Libya. As originally issued the uniform included a lightweight heavy denim (linen) tunic, similar in cut to the ordinary 1936 pattern service tunic except that the collar was open in style with fashioned revers. Long trousers (and breeches for the officers) in the same material were supplied and worn with high front-laced boots (almost knee-height) made of leather and green canvas. A matching drill shirt and tie were worn. With the trousers ordinary ankle boots, or sometimes ankle boots and gaiters, could be worn instead of the high lace-up canvas boots. Insignia and badges on the tunic matched the style of those worn with the field grey service dress, but they were in a coppery-brown weave on a tan background rather than in silver-grey on a field grey background. In addition to long trousers or breeches, ordinary shorts were issued in the same denim material. The tropical dress was produced in a very light sage green or sand colour, but it was very susceptible to change both from

weathering and washing so actual shades varied widely, from a definite greenish tinge to a completely washed-out bleached linen shade.

A special tropical pith sun helmet was originally issued with the tropical clothing outfit and it was widely worn in the opening weeks of the North African campaign in 1941. On this helmet the shield in national colours and the Wehrmacht eagle badge were worn on the side in corresponding positions to those on the steel helmet. The helmet proved uncomfortable and unwieldy so it was soon discarded, replaced by a Feldmütze in light drill material, the shape being based on that of the mountain cap. The officer's version had silver piping round the crown. On the front of the cap was worn the national emblem and Reichskokarde. A lightweight drill version of the 1938 pattern Feldmütze was also produced though it was not so widely worn as the peaked Feldmütze.

There were numerous variations. The high laced canvas boots were considered cumbersome and many men discarded them, preferring the ordinary ankle boots. Others cut down the tops of

these high boots to reduce them to ankle boot-height. Sometimes long trousers were cut down to short length. With shorts in wear the legs were clad either in ankle-length socks and boots, long stockings and ankle boots, or long stockings with the high-laced tropical boots. As the desert campaign progressed, informal and comfortable clothes were often worn. Non-standard jerseys and scarves were common, and regulations were not rigidly adhered to. The steel helmet was painted sand-yellow, sometimes with sand thrown over the wet paint to render the surface completely flat. A helmet cover from light canvas or white sheeting was also to be seen.

The lightweight tropical uniform was popular and in the early part of 1943 it was standardised for wear on all southern fronts, including Italy,

Plate 117: *A young Obergefreiter of the Afrika Korps wearing the lightweight forage cap and service tunic. He also has the infantry assault badge and Iron Cross 2nd Class.*

Plate 118: *Gen von Thoma after surrender to the British. He wears the standard lightweight tropical uniform with general's insignia in regulation style.*

Plate 119: *Afrika Korps Unteroffizier in the lightweight tropical uniform, wearing a sand-coloured cloth or canvas helmet cover and carrying a MP38 with the appropriate ammunition pouches.*

Plate 120: *An Afrika Korps leutnant (right) followed by a private, leaves a Junkers Ju52 demonstrating 'shirts and shorts' order for the hottest weather. On the ground is a field grey rucksack — favoured by the DAK — and a rolled Zeltbahn/blanket 'horseshoed' over it.*

the Balkans, and the Crimea. Some units in Normandy and NW Europe in summer 1944 were wearing this uniform too. The colour for southern European use was changed to light reed green and the badges for the standard field grey service dress were worn with it. There was considerable variation with this uniform. All the types of headwear could be seen with it, but sometimes it was worn in mixed style, such as the lightweight denim tunic with ordinary field grey service trousers, or the field grey 1943 pattern tunic with denim reed green trousers. The lightweight Feldmütze was also issued with this suit, again in light reed green.

91

CAMOUFLAGE CLOTHING

The Heer did not issue camouflage clothing on such an extensive scale as the Waffen-SS which used it from early in the war. A standard camouflage garment, however, was the Zeltbahn — a camouflage quarter-shelter, which was a poncho (cape) of triangular shape 8ft 3in x 8ft 3in x 6ft 3in (247.5cm x 247.5cm x 187.5cm) in size. It was designed so that four Zeltbahn could be buttoned together to form a tent. A single Zeltbahn could also provide a rudimentary bivouac for its owner, could be used as a groundsheet, or could be worn as a cape by the owner inserting his head through a flapped slit in the middle. The hanging ends of the cape were then secured together and a motorcycle rider or cyclist could strap the ends round his legs and waist to stop them from fouling the wheels. The illustration shows the principle of this garment. When not in use the Zeltbahn was folded up and secured with the owner's personal equipment. The Zeltbahn was made in proofed drill material and was finished in a spring/summer pattern (mainly green) on one side, and an autumn/winter camouflage on the other (mainly brown).

The main Army camouflage style was the so-called 'splinter' pattern made up of jagged-edge long segments in various shades of green and brown. A lesser used alternative was a 'water'

pattern where the segments of colour were run into each other producing a 'watery' effect where they merged. This pattern was also 'flecked' overall in a contrasting colour, usually black or dark brown. These differed completely from Waffen-SS 'Dappled' camouflage patterns.

Camouflage helmet covers and smocks were introduced during 1942 and these were almost certainly inspired by the widespread use of similar garments by the Waffen-SS. The standard camouflage patterns described above were used for the material, mainly 'splinter' type from pictorial evidence. The helmet cover was shaped to fit under the helmet rim and carried loops for affixing local foliage. The Army camouflage smock was cut full, had a lace-up neck, no collar and cuffs. It had side slits for access to the tunic pockets underneath. The smock was reversible with 'splinter' or 'water' pattern on the outside and a white inside for wear in the snow.

In the latter part of the war a camouflage suit was introduced, this being merely a camouflage printed version of the lightweight drill tropical uniform with trousers and tunic, the latter being usually worn with an open turned-down collar. This suit was not widely issued and it was possible to see it worn in various combinations, such as the camouflage tunic with ordinary field grey trousers, and so on. 'Splinter' and 'water' pattern garments existed.

Various other camouflage items were used. Combat units in the field commonly utilised local foliage in their helmets to provide an added aid to concealment. A favourite method of holding the foliage to a helmet was by means of cycle inner-tube strips stretched round the helmet. Webbing straps were officially issued for the same purpose. Net or sacking covers were alternatives for helmets. A camouflage version of the Einheitsfeldmütze saw limited issue as did camouflaged face masks for snipers and special troops. The face masks came in either camouflage or white cloth material depending on season. Also recorded in the Normandy campaign was a 'string vest' type garment worn over the tunic by some units. Local foliage was secured in the netting to give a 'walking bush' effect to the wearer. Giving a similar degree of body camouflage was camouflage body apron, a pinafore-like garment.

Plate 121: *A soldier wearing the Zeltbahn during the 1939 campaign in Poland.*

121

Plate 122: *Soldiers wearing the Zeltbahn in 1943 and with netting on their helmets for the attachment of camouflage.*

Plate 123: *The Zeltbahn laid out with the personal equipment for a kit inspection.*

92

Plate 124: *The method of donning the Zeltbahn, and four joined together to make a tent.*

with an aperture for the head. It hung down the body front and rear and was secured at the sides by tapes. Finished in the 'water' pattern camouflage, it was full enough to cover personal equipment. The Zeltbahn, a much larger garment, was also sometimes worn as a camouflage aid. Finally there was a mosquito net in fine green mesh material large enough to fit over the helmet and hang down all round to cover the wearer's face and shoulders. It was issued in areas where there was a risk of mosquito bites and, though primarily protective, it was also used as a camouflage aid to conceal the face. Sometimes it was worn round the neck like a scarf and could also be seen pulled up to cover the nose to form a mask for camouflage purposes.

Plate 125: *An Army Flak gun crew in the Army camouflage smock (see also Plate 102) with the 'splinter' pattern side outwards. Note the netting on helmets with attached foliage, seen here in the late war period.*

Plate 126: *The green mosquito net worn over the helmet by a machine gunner on the Russian Front in 1943.*

94

e most numerous variations in Army camou-
ge clothing were for winter wear. In the early
rt of the war — the first two winters — the
ow camouflage dress was of an extemporised
ture. White sheets fastened round the neck
d/or helmet were the simplest form. There was
o a white coverall which had sleeves and a
od to cover the helmet. This coverall was loose
ing, for wear over personal equipment, and
ched below the knees. A more abbreviated
orter version of this garment without the hood
s also issued. With this garment the helmet
s either painted white or was covered with
ite sheeting held in place by tyre inner tubes
the webbing camouflage straps. Later in the
r more sophisticated snow camouflage gar-
nts were produced. Most important was a two-
ce coverall suit consisting of smock and
users, the smock having a loose hood. An
uivalent garment was a one-piece coverall suit
ich was like a loose-fitting set of overalls in
pearance, with a loose hood which could be
lled up over the helmet. Both these latter gar-
nts were intended for wear over the service
ess and they were loose enough to cover the
arer's personal equipment. It was possible,
wever, to wear the personal equipment over
coveralls if desired. These were linen gar-
nts of good quality.

The various snow coveralls, while adding
another layer over service dress, gave only mini-
mal extra protection against winter cold. They
were primarily for camouflage only. It was in the
first winter of the campaign in Russia, 1941-42,
that the need for purpose-designed winter clothing became only too apparent. In time for the following winter, 1942-43, a new winter uniform

127

te 127: *White snow camouflage coverall, with
oured identification strips on sleeve.*

te 128: *White helmet covers used in the Norwegian
mpaign in April 1940. Wool gloves are being worn
th greatcoats and the nearest man appears to have
ur collar on his coat.*

128

Plate 129: *White coverall being worn by a detail in NW Europe in 1944, carrying hot food to forward troops.*

Plate 130: *Sentries in Poland during January 1940, wearing the animal skin winter coat, toques, heavy gauntlets and (right) the straw-filled winter boots. Both also wear the 1916 pattern helmet.*

was designed and in production. This was a two-piece item consisting of trousers with webbing suspenders (braces) and a front-buttoning smock. Two layers of windproof and waterproof cloth with an internal quilted wool lining and a fitted hood were used, with drawstrings to pull tight the waist band, waist and hood. The suit was completely reversible, being finished in white one side for snow camouflage and in 'water' or 'splinter' camouflage pattern on the other for cold weather conditions in non-snowy conditions. Some suits were issued in field grey or mouse grey finish instead of the camouflage finish. On the arms of the white side of this smock, provision was made (in the form of small buttons 20cm from the shoulder) for fastening coloured cloth identity strips which were used to distinguish friend from foe when both sides were wearing white in the snow. For security reasons the colours were changed as required, usually daily.

There were a number of extemporised forms of cold weather clothing, the most common being a modified greatcoat. Fur collars added over the fitted collar were quite commonly seen and there was a version of the greatcoat with added fur lining. There was also a version of the greatcoat with an added hood and various quilted inner linings for greatcoats and trousers were also produced. Winter headwear included conventional fur caps with fur crowns and turn-down side-flaps, and a similar-looking hat which was actually a Feldmütze with a field grey wool overlay with fur lining added.

Plate 131: *The two-piece padded winter suit, worn white side outwards, with coloured identification strips on the sleeves.*

Plate 132: *The two-piece padded winter suit worn camouflage side outwards. It was also produced in plain field grey on this side.*

In the early part of the war, prior to the Russian campaign, the most commonly seen winter garment was a full length sheepskin coat which was mostly issued to sentries and duty men in very cold weather. This coat had a high fur collar. Also issued at this time were sheepskin mittens, and leather straw-lined overboots. In addition to all this, there was a standard issue of gloves, scarf and toque, all in heavy field grey knit. The toque was designed to be used in several ways, the most common being as a head-covering under a cap or helmet. Officers mainly had brown leather gloves but could also be seen with the field grey wool gloves; private of purchase gloves could give other variations.

Men in motorcycle companies and battalions were issued with a special loose-fitting long coat in rubberised grey-green material. It was double-breasted and buttoned up to the neck, but it could also be buttoned close round each leg to keep it clear of the engine parts. A lighter version also existed for summer wear or theatres where the lightweight tropical uniform was worn.

Plate 133: *An officer wearing the reversible two-piece winter suit, white side outwards. He also wears the old-style officer's service cap.*

Plate 134: *The two-piece winter suit being worn field grey side outwards by a Panzerfaust gunner towards the end of the war.*

Plate 135: *The two-piece reversible winter suit worn by a signaller white side outwards without the identification strips. Note the ordinary waistbelt worn outside, a typical variation.*

Plate 136: *The army windproof suit worn tan or field ~~gr~~ey side outwards by a mortar crew. Also shown are ~~th~~e padded winter gloves. The nearest man wears a ~~to~~que over the Einheitsfeldmütze and his ears, a ~~ty~~pical cold-weather procedure.*

Plate 137: *An assault gun crew wearing the army windproof suit white side outwards. See also Plate 133 and 102.*

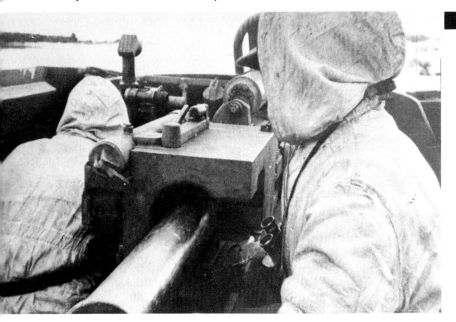

For Parade Dress the German soldier was issued with a new style of uniform tunic (Waffenrock) from the end of June 1935 which was superior in cut, material and insignia to the service dress tunic. Trousers of matching quality were also issued. This Parade Dress uniform was used on all review and ceremonial occasions, and by sentries and duty men on formal occasions. With the peaked cap (Schimmütze) and shoes or ankle boots, it was also used as a walking -out dress. Officers wore a Waffenrock and trousers of almost identical style, and all ranks had the same insignia and decoration variations as noted with the service dress. With the outbreak of war in September 1939 the issue of this uniform was suspended, though it was still occasionally seen in wear during the war years on special occasions (such as weddings) by those who still had the prewar issue.

The Waffenrock was made in superior field grey material, was single-breasted with eight white metal buttons, and closed up to the neck. Turned-up 'Swedish'-style cuffs were faced with

Plate 138: *The Waffenrock of an infantry Unteroffizier, showing regimental number in gilt.*

Plate 139: *Detail of cuff decoration, infantry Unteroffizier Waffenrock.*

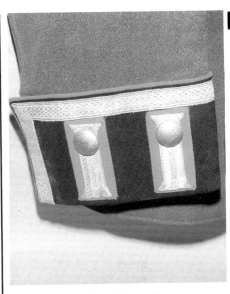

Plate 140: *The Waffenrock of an artillery Unteroffizier, all Waffenfarbe piping being red.*

Plate 141: *Detail of insignia on artillery Unteroffizier Waffenrock.*

Plate 142: *Detail of cuff decoration on artillery Unteroffizier Waffenrock.*

cade weave was in aluminium colour with white metal buckle featuring the Wehrmac eagle in an oakleaf surround. The backing mat rial was in dark bottle green. For generals t weave was gilt, and for Directors of Music t backing colour was bright red.

Officers also wore Aiguilletes (shoulder cord with parade dress. These were ornate plaite cords attached below the right shoulder strap an looped over the breast to secure behind the se ond button of the tunic. For generals the Aigu letes were woven in gilt cord, and for other off cers aluminium cord. Adjutants had a mo elaborate decoration with two hanging cords an ferrules attached. Directors of Music had a brig red silk thread woven between the cords match the decoration of the dress belt. Aiguillet were also worn with the service dress tunic c ceremonial occasions and parades. They cou also be worn with the special armoured servi dress, either black or field grey, on these occ sions. With service dress they were not worn c other occasions, with the exception of staff off cers (including adjutants) who wore them to ind cate their office.

Another ceremonial item, carrying on a lor German tradition, was the Portapee — an adorn ment for swords, sabres and bayonets. The Po tapee was essentially an ornate knot (or ball) on strap which was tied around the hilt of an edge weapon. The Portapee was specifically the nam reserved for the knots used on officers' sword and daggers; the similar decoration used o NCOs' bayonets was the Troddel, and on th sabre the Faustriemen. All were similar in con struction, though the dagger Portapee was longe Originally the weave and cording was done in si ver wire, but from November 1935 this wa changed to aluminium wire, and from Januar 1942 it was changed to artificial silk. From Apr 1943 issue was terminated, but those still in po session continued to be worn. Portapees (an equivalents) were worn on all ceremonial an parade occasions, for walking out and when o duties in barracks. They were not worn on can paign and for that reason are less familiar th most other German uniform items. The rules fc the patterns and weave were immensely comple with specific colours in the weave indicating a

dark bottle green material as was the collar (and shoulder straps for NCOs and enlisted men). Litzen patches were carried on the collar (as for service dress tunics) but on the Waffenrock there were cuff patches similar in style to the collar Litzen. Waffenfarbe piping 2mm thick edged the shoulder straps, collar, the front of the tunic, the cuffs and two tunic flaps on the rear skirt. Waffenfarbe was also worked into the collar Litzen and the cuff patches. There were no front pockets in the tunic but there were two concealed pockets in the rear skirts in line with the flaps. Waffenfarbe piping also ran down the outer seams of the parade dress trousers.

A variation on the Waffenrock was designed for the elite 'Grossdeutschland' infantry regiment in September 1939. This had much longer collar Litzen patches and 'French' cuffs, but owing to the outbreak of war this variation was never actually issued.

With the Waffenrock, NCOs and enlisted men wore the standard service belt and equipment. Originally officers conformed to this, but from July 1937 an elaborate brocade and velvet dress belt was specified for wear with parade dress. When wear of the Waffenrock and parade dress was suspended with the outbreak of war, this dress belt was also worn with the service dress tunic on parades and formal occasions. The bro-

individual's battalion, company, seniority of regiment, and in some cases historical links. To give a simplified example the four companies of an infantry battalion had the crown (of the knot) colouring in white, red, bright yellow and corn-flower blue respectively (from 1-4); the actual battalion within the regiment was then indicated by the colouring in the slide behind the knot in white, red, yellow and cornflower blue respectively (from 1-4).

REICHSHEER SERVICE DRESS

In the early years of the Third Reich era, the old pattern service dress of the Reichsheer was being worn. The service dress tunic had turnback cuffs, a patch pocket on each breast and a diagonal pocket with buttoned flap on each front skirt. There were eight front buttons. The pocket flaps were of the three-pointed type as were also used in the later 1936 pattern tunic. Though marching boots were to be seen, a common form of wear was ankle boots with black leather buckled gaiters. This tunic continued in wear into decreasing numbers into the Third Reich era, but was rapidly replaced with the 1936 pattern tunic from 1936. However, many officers, who had tailored versions of the tunic, continued to wear it throughout the World War 2 period. The easy identification comes from the diagonally sloped pocket flaps in the front skirts instead of the patch pockets of the 1936 pattern tunic. Nazi insignia was added to the Reichsheer service dress from the earliest days of the Third Reich. The new helmet markings (national colours and eagle with swastika) were ordered from 15 Ma 1933, as was the new-style cap badge featuri the Reichskokarde. Later the Hoheitabzeic breast badge was ordered to be worn. *(For il trations see section 1 of this book.)*

FATIGUE AND DRILL DRESS

A prewar issue suit was the white denim fatigue dress, worn for drills, exercises and dirty work. It consisted of rather loose fitting trousers and a loose single-breasted jacket. After 1940 it was rarely issued, but the garments continued in use. Sometimes the trousers were seen in wear with the normal field grey tunic in the field while engineer and construction companies, or vehicle mechanics, might wear all or part of the suit on duties like bridge construction, road building, or vehicle maintenance. The wartime replacem for the fatigue dress was the field grey ove suit.

Plate 145: *The white fatigue dress being worn by n building blockhouses on the Russian Front in May 1942. Note boots worn under and outside trousers, and the men behind wearing greatcoats over the white fatigue dress.*

Plate 146: *Tank and assault gun crews receive mail from home while undertaking maintenance work. They are wearing the field grey overall fatigue dress.*

Plate 147: *The field grey overall fatigue suit worn with marching boots and the Feldmütze by a tank soldier.*

Plate 148: *Engineers building a bridge. Both the nearest men are wearing the white fatigue jacket but with field grey service trousers.*

MISCELLANEOUS GARMENTS

There were a number of items of dress that do not fit easily into other categories. Among these were the officers' white summer tunic which was a prewar issue for walking out or informal occasions. The original Reichsheer pattern was cut like the Reichsheer service tunic but was made in white linen. In 1937 a new pattern was issued that was cut in the same style as the 1936 pattern service dress tunic. Both types could be seen in wear. This tunic was for wear on prescribed occasions in hot weather between 1 April and 30 September in place of the usual tunic. Also occasionally seen in wear by officers was a field grey front-buttoned cloak and a privately purchased raincoat.

A garment unique to army chaplains and bis ops was a single-breasted field grey frockco which had a stand-up collar and turnback cufl It was of typical clerical cut similar to black coa of this type worn by civilian priests. Chaplai had white metal silver-grey buttons and bisho and gilt buttons. Violet Waffenfarbe piping w carried on the front flap of the coat, around t collar and round the top of the cuffs.

The standard issue of sports clothing for phy ical training was a white cotton vest with bla Hoheitabzeichen national emblem on the fror and black cotton shorts. Brown leath lightweight sports shoes were issued for we with this gear.

ARMY OFFICIALS

Army officials (Beamten) were, in effect, civil servants in uniform carrying out military administrative duties. They were uniformed as officers, or in some cases NCOs, with ranks equivalent to those in the army. The regulations for officials were complex and subtle, with distinctions and ranks related to career status. Among specialisations of Beamten were librarians, teachers, forestry service, food supply, archivists, translators, meteorologists and vehicle supply specialists, but there were many more. The Waffenfarbe for Beamten was dark green, but many branches had secondary colours, too, which might be worked into insignia. The Litzen on the collar patches, which in some cases had distinctive patterns, was an obvious variation from the army itself. A good example was a Beamte with equivalent rank to a general. While having the general's style collar braid, the backing was in dark green rather than the bright red, unique to an army general. The rank badges matched those of the army,

but the officials were ranked descriptive of the specialisation. A full list would run to mar pages but, as an example an archivist with t equivalent rank of a Colonel (Oberst) would l known as a Heersarchivdirektor while the equi alent to a Lt-Col would be a Oberheeresarchivr a Major a Heeresarchivrat, and so on. Most, b not all, Beamten had a 'HV' cypher on the shoulder straps (HV - Heeresverwaltung - arn administration).

A further category of personnel who wo army uniform and had officer ranks and stat but did not hold commissions were specialis who were classed as Sonderführer. These we mostly interpreters, reporters, or doctors rank as Hauptmann (Captain), Major or Lieutenar They wore officers' service dress, but had distin tive blue-grey Waffenfarbe and shoulder stra with small chevrons woven in the nation colours.

AWARDS AND DECORATIONS

For skill at arms, distinguished combat service, arduous campaigns, or brave conduct there were many awards, distinctions, or insignia. The most important of these are illustrated.

Marksmanship
In the Reichsheer, soldiers who scored at various levels on the range and in tests were awarded marksmanship stripes to indicate the level of skill they reached. The stripe was a length of aluminium braid across with a dark green stripe through the middle. There were grades for small arms and also for machine guns and anti-tank

guns, AA and infantry guns. The higher grad had wider stripes. These were worn on the le cuff and were awarded to privates and NCC only, through officers commissioned from t ranks could retain the stripes. A qualified shar shooter had a single chevron worn below t marksmanship stripes. In June 1936 this syste was replaced by the award of a markmansh lanyard woven in aluminium cord and wo from the right shoulder to the second button the tunic, on parade or service dress only. The featured shields at the top of the lanyard with Wehrmacht shield in the lower grades and

shield with oakleaf surround in higher grades. The highest grades of all had the lanyard and shield in gilt colour. Infantry had cords with acorns to indicate grades and artillery and armoured troops had miniature shells replacing the acorns. From October 1938, when armoured troops were given marksmanship lanyards, the shield on the lanyard incorporated a tank design.

Tank Destruction Badge
Issued from March 1942, this was awarded to any soldier who destroyed an enemy tank single-handed without using an anti-tank weapon. The badge was 8.5cm wide and 3cm deep and was made in aluminium-braided cloth with black edging top and bottom, for the silver class; for the

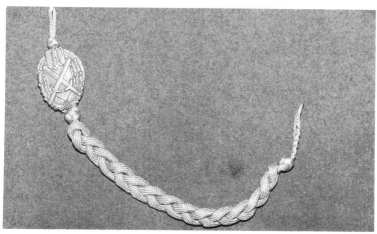

150

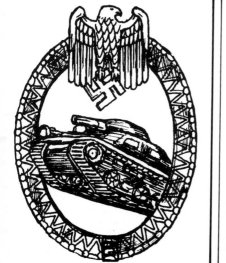

Plate 149: *Marksmanship cuff stripes of the Reichsheer, discontinued in 1936. The chevron, worn with or without the stripes, indicated a sharpshooter.*

Plate 150: *Army marksmanship lanyard, replacing the stripes from 1936. The original pattern had a Wehrmacht eagle only on the shield. The version shown was introduced in 1939. This is the basic award without 'acorns' for higher grades of skill.*

Plate 151: *The alternative lanyard shield for armoured troops' marksmanship proficiency. This design replaced the shield on the lanyard shown in Plate 150.*

107

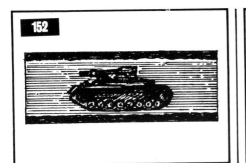

higher gold class the braiding was in gilt colour. A bronze tank symbol was superimposed in both classes. The silver award was made for each tank destroyed up to a maximum of five. For the destruction of five tanks in total the gold award replaced it. Thus one gold class badge indicated that the man had destroyed five enemy tanks. he had destroyed three enemy tanks, for example, he would wear three silver badges. If he destroyed six enemy tanks he would wear one gold class badge plus one silver class badge. The badge was worn on the upper arm in service dress or equivalent combat dress. Though introduced in 1942 it was also awarded retrospectively for tank destruction claims back to the start of the Russian campaign, 22 June 1941.

Plate 152: *Tank destruction badge.*

Plate 153: *Low-flying aircraft destruction badge.*

Plate 154: *Close combat clasp.*

Plate 155: *Tank Badge.*

Plate 156: *Belt buckle with 'Gott Mit Uns' motto.*

Plate 157: *Left to right: Partisan Warfare Badge, Assault Badge for Other Arms, Infantry Assault Badge (all worn on left breast).*

Low Flying Aircraft Destruction Badge

In all respects this matched the Tank Destruction Badge, being awarded in silver and gold classes for the same totals destroyed. The silver class had black-coloured metal aircraft superimposed and the gold class had a gilt metal aircraft. The weapon used had to be any small arm or small calibre gun to a maximum calibre of 12mm. The badge was worn on the upper right arm. As it was promulgated late in the war, in January 1945, few, if any, were actually awarded.

Sniper's Badge (Scharfschützen-abzeichen)

This was a cloth badge featuring an eagle's head framed at the bottom by oak leaves. Oval in shape, with the head in black and the leaves in green weave, the third class version had plain

Plate 158: *An Unteroffizier wearing the lightweight tunic and decorated with two tank destruction badges, the close combat clasp, and infantry assault badge (plus probably a wound badge, though not distinct). He carries the MP38 sub-machine gun (late war period).*

109

Plate 159: *Feldwebel with two tank destruction badges and wearing an Iron Cross 1st Class.*

Plate 160: *An Unteroffizier in 1940 with infantry assault badge and ribbon of the Iron Cross 2nd Class.*

edges, the second class had a silver border, and the first class award had a gilt border. It was to be worn on the right cuff of service dress above any other cuff insignia. Awarded from August 1944 only to those actually deployed as snipers, it is another rare badge.

Close Combat Clasp
Awarded for distinguished frontline combat, this was a metal badge featuring a crossed bayonet and hand grenade with oakleaf background. The silver class was aluminium colour and the gold class was gilt. It was worn on the left breast matching the height of the national emblem on the right breast.

Infantry Assault Badge (Infanterie-Sturmabzeichen)
This was a white metal badge with aluminium finish featuring a rifle, eagle and oakleaf laurel. It was awarded for three successful attacks on three different days and was worn on the left breast.

Plate 161: *Medal ribbons as normally worn on the left breast of the tunic.*

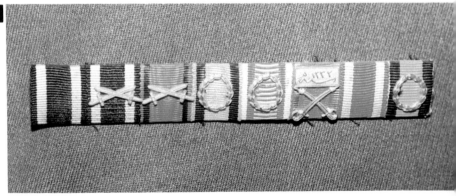

Assault Badge for Other Arms (Sturmabzeichen anderer Waffengattungen)

This was the equivalent to the Infantry Assault Badge awarded to branches other than the infantry for participating in three successful attacks on three successive days. It was in aluminium colour white metal, worn on the left breast. The design featured a crossed grenade and bayonet surmounted by an eagle and with oakleaf surround.

Tank Badge (Panzerkampfwagen-Abzeichen)

Cast in bronze, this badge featured a tank within an oakleaf surround. Initially it was awarded for three successful attacks on different days, but from July 1943 extra grades were issued for 25, 50, 75 and 100 actions with the figure carried in the knot at the bottom of the oakleaf surround.

Wound Badge (Verwundeten-Abzeichen)

This small badge consisted of two crossed bayonets below a steel helmet bearing a swastika, with an oakleaf surround. It was awarded in three classes — 3rd class, painted black, for one or two wounds; 2nd class, in silver, for three or four wounds; and 1st class, in gold (gilt), for more than four wounds. It was worn on the left breast pocket of the service tunic.

Partisan Warfare Badge

This badge, consisting of a dagger plunged into a nest of vipers, was awarded to all forces taking an active part in anti-partisan operations. It was in aluminium-colour white metal and worn on the left breast.

Iron Cross (Eisernes Kreuz)

A detailed coverage of German war medals is beyond the scope of this book, but some mention will be made of those most commonly seen. The Iron Cross was awarded for outstanding service and for conspicuous bravery in the face of the enemy. The Iron Cross 1st Class was worn (cross only) on the left breast pocket of the service

Plate 162: *Medals as worn on parade and formal occasions. This group includes the Iron Cross, two long service awards (with national emblems on ribbon), an entry to Prague commemorative medal, and two pre-Third Reich awards at right.*

dress. The more common Iron Cross, 2nd Class, was indicated on service dress, or combat dress equivalent, by wearing the red/white/black ribbon diagonally through the second button position on the tunic. The Knight's Cross of the Iron Cross was worn round the neck close up to the collar at the throat.

War Merit Cross (Kreigsverdienstkreuz)

This was the equivalent to the Iron Cross for meritorious service not involving enemy action. It was awarded with swords for actions involving the enemy.

German Cross (Deutsche Kreuz)

This was instituted in September 1941 to fall between the award of the Iron Cross 1st Class and the Knight's Cross. Despite its name it was not a cross in shape. It consisted an eight-pointed star about 6cm across. A swastika on a dull silver background is carried in the centre with a gold or silver laurel surround. There were also silver and gold classes for exceptional service. This cross was worn, without ribbons, on the right breast.

Other medals

Other medals were worn in the form of medal ribbons on the left breast in service dress, but the actual medals would be worn with parade dress and on formal or ceremonial occasions. Among medals which might be seen were the Iron Cross in various grades, War Merit Cross in various grades, Winter Campaign in Russia 1941-42, War Merit Medal, Long Service Award in various grades, Commemorative Medals covering various actions such as the occupation of Czechoslovakia.

For certain major campaigns or actions, special commemorative insignia were issued to participating personnel. These awards took the form, variously, of cuff titles, arm shields or medals. The most important included the following.

'Afrika Korps' cuff title introduced in July 1941 for all members of the Deutsche Afrika Korps. (See cover illustration for style)

'Afrika' cuff title January 1943 replacement for the previous cuff title. The word AFRIKA was woven in silver-grey with palm tree symbols each side of the word in the same colour, on a brown backing.

'Kreta' cuff title Issued from October 1942 for anyone who took part in the invasion of Crete. The decoration consisted of the word KRETA flanked by acanthus leaves and a woven border, all in yellow on a white backing.

'Spain' cuff title This was a cuff title awarded to any soldier who had served as a volunteer in the Condor Legion for the Spanish Civil War. It was lettered1936 SPANIEN 1939 in gold lettering on a red backing with gold wove edging.

'Metz' cuff title This was awarded to all who participated in the defence of Metz, July-September 1944. It was lettered METZ 1944 with silver-coloured lettering and edge woven on a black backing.

'Kurland' cuff title This was awarded in March 1945 for soldiers besieged in the Courland area, Latvia, where the fighting was heavy. It was lettered KURLAND in black with two shields on a silver-grey backing. Probably very few were actually issued.

With the exception of the Spanish cuff title, which was worn on the right cuff, all the above were worn on the left cuff and could also be worn on the greatcoat cuff.

'Crimea' shield This was awarded to all Wehrmacht members who were involved in the Crimea campaign between 21 September 1941 and 4 July 1942. The requirement for the award was taking part in a battle, being wounded in action, or serving in the area for at least three months. The shield featured a bas-relief of the Crimean peninsula, lettered 'Krim 1941-1942'. It was worn on the upper left arm.

'Kholm' shield This was awarded to all who took part in the defence of Kholm, south of Lake Ilmen in the USSR, from mid-January to mid-April 1942. The design featured a German eagle over an Iron Cross, lettered 'Kholm 1942'. It was worn on the upper left arm.

'Narvik' shield This was awarded to all Wehrmacht personnel who took part in the Battle of Narvik in April 1940. The design featured an Edelweiss (mountain flower), an anchor and a German eagle and swastika. The army version was in silver finish and was worn on the upper left sleeve.

'East Medal' This was a special medal struck for Wehrmacht members who served on the Eastern Front, November 1941 to April 1942. Apart from the medal itself, the insignia was denoted by a dark red ribbon with white/black/white stripes.

DEUTSCHER VOLKSSTURM

The Deutscher Volkssturm (German People's Militia) had only one common uniform item, an identifying armband worn on the left arm. The official version had white lettering on a black background, with a white national emblem often (but not always) adjacent to the lettering. The upper and lower edges were in red, thus completing the national colours. The wording on the armband was 'Deutscher Volkssturm Wehrmacht' with the final word forming a second line. Sometimes the word 'Wehrmacht' was omitted. This was particularly more likely on the locally produced versions of the armband most of which were in plain white (or other light colours) with the wording printed on in black. The national emblem, when carried, was also in black on these armbands. There was considerable variation. Members of the Volkssturm had to provide their own uniforms and small arms, but in practice the

Gau organisations used stocks of old party clothing or appealed locally to get together an assortment of uniform items. There was a mixture of civilian clothing with armbands right through to old Heer or Luftwaffe uniforms more or less complete. In between could be seen uniforms made up from various sources, such as Hitler Youth caps, SA shirts and Luftwaffe trousers, or similar non-matching combinations. Many members favoured uniform items of some sort, as being captured in civilian clothing only could be risky. Similarly old SA uniform items were less popular than others, for few Volkssturm members relished being mistaken for party members if captured.

The 'regulation' uniform for the Volkssturm where procurable, was the same as the army service dress, but rank was indicated only on black collar patches. There were no shoulder straps

and the Volkssturm armband was the only other identification. The national emblem worn on the right breast was the army style version.

Rank organisation and identification was simple:

• *Volkssturmman (private)*	Plain black collar patches
• *Gruppenführer (corporal)*	Black collar patches with single diamond (aluminium colour)
• *Zügführer (sergeant)*	Black collar patches with two diamonds diagonally
• *Kompanieführer (captain)*	Black collar patches with three diamonds diagonally
• *Batallionsführer (Lt-Col)*	Black collar patches with four diamonds

(Rank equivalents are approximate)

Plate 163: *Volkssturmman with obsolete anti-tank rifle, and in civilian clothes with 'Deutscher Volkssturm' armband.*

WOMEN AUXILIARIES

The original body of women helpers, the Corps of Army Signal Auxiliaries (Nachrichtenhelferinnen des Heeres) wore a stone grey service dress consisting of a double-breasted coat-style tunic with two flapped breast pockets, a pleated skirt, a white shirt, black tie, wool cardigan and low-heel black shoes. Wool stockings were issued for winter wear and silk stockings and white ankle socks for summer wear. Wool trousers could be issued in cold weather areas. Headwear was a Feldmütze of 1938 pattern with Waffenfarbe piping (lemon yellow). A black leather shoulder bag was

issued as part of the uniform and there was a greatcoat of civilian-type cut. There was also a raincape. In hot areas there was also an extra summer issue of lightweight white skirt and white short-sleeve shirt.

Apart from national insignia of standard army type worn on the right breast, the specialist 'blitz' army signaller badge (lemon yellow on a dark bottle green patch) was worn on the left arm and on the left side of the Feldmütze. It was also worn in the form of a brooch on the tie, or at the throat of the shirt if the tie was not worn.

For everyday work duties a service shirt in light grey was issued, this having the Hohenabzeichen national emblem on the right breast. There was also a light grey or light brown overall work dress with button front, side pockets and the national emblem on the right breast. Later in the war a simplified single-breasted tunic coat was issued, but it did not supplant the original issue.

When the Corps of Staff Auxiliaries was formed they wore the same uniform but without the signaller badges. The Women Horse Breakers wore the later war period single-breasted tunic and grey riding breeches with black leather riding boots. The Feldmütze was originally worn, but this was soon replaced with a version of the peaked Einheitsfeldmütze. The Corps of Welfare Auxiliaries wore German Red Cross uniforms or civilian clothes with armbands lettered for 'Deutsches Wehrmacht'.

Uniforms were issued in the first instance to personnel serving in occupied countries and most women of any branch serving in Germany itself wore civilian clothing with only an armband (and usually a brooch) to indicate their status. Typical armband lettering for staff auxiliaries would read 'Stabshelferin des Heeres'. Later in the war there was wider uniform issue within Germany or, alternatively, issue of the overall work dress only.

Ranks and insignia for women auxiliaries varied over the war years. Later in the war new ranks and insignia were introduced but the typical range was as follows:

- *Nachrichtenhelferin (private)* No insignia
- *Oberhelferin (corporal)* Yellow chevron on arm below signal badge
- *Unterführerin (sergeant)* Yellow chevron with two diamond
- *Führerin (lieutenant)* Yellow twist piping collar, cap and signal badge, and ornamented on brooch
- *Oberführerin (major)* Gold twist cord arranged as above

Later, further ranks were introduced including:
- *Vorhelferin (lance corporal)* Single diamond below signaller badge
- *Stabsführerin* Gold chevron with gold twist cord on collar
- *Oberstabsführerin* Gold chevron with single diamond above it on collar, with gold twist cord on collar edge, as above

The Führerin badge was changed to a chevron and the Oberführerin to a chevron with single diamond above it, and all ranks from Führerin upwards then wore the rank badge on the corner of each collar only.

(Equivalent ranks given above are an indication of status only, and were not official comparisons. *For illustrations see section 2 of this book.*)

PAYBOOK (SOLDBUCH)

All personnel were issued with a pocket-size paybook which also acted as an identity book. It was strongly bound with tough linen-like paper to make it durable. It contained all personal details of the holder, including pay group, medical details, physical details, record of service, record of leave, next-of-kin, a copy of identity tag lettering and a photograph. It was quite usual to carry a driving licence or other personal documents inside this as well.

The book was carried at all times except when taking part in a raid or attack.

Plate 164: *Soldbuch open at first spread.*

Plate 165: *Soldbuch cover, plus civil driving licence carried inside.*

IDENTITY DISCS

ll personnel were issued on joining with a zinc val-shaped tag divided into two halves by a perpration. The details were duplicated on each alf. In the event of death in action or on service, he lower half of the tag was broken off and eturned to the home depot, and the remaining .alf of the tag was buried with the body. The riginal type included unit identification and blood group, but in the later type this was replaced by a field post office number. This meant it gave no information away if the man was captured or the body was recovered by the enemy. But to the Germans themselves, the information could be retrieved by referring this number back to central records.

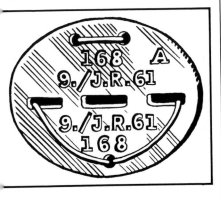

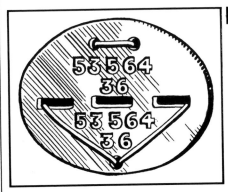

Plate 166: *Early pattern identity disc indicating 9th Company of 61st Infantry Regiment, personal number 168 and blood group A. Note horizontal perforation.*

Plate 167: *Later type identity disc carrying only personal number, 36, plus field post five-digit code number.*

CHAPLAINS

Chaplains were officially Beamten. The chaplain was known as a Heeresgeistliche, and military bishops were known as Feldbischöfe. They wore the same service dress as officers but without shoulder straps. The chaplain had violet Waffen-farbe piping and bishops had gold piping. Both wore gold chains with crosses carried round the neck. For Protestants the cross was plain and for Roman Catholics it featured the figure of Christ. On the peaked cap a small cross was carried below the national emblem and above the Reichs-kokarde. For formal wear there was a single-breasted grey frockcoat of clerical appearance as noted in the section on greatcoats. From the time of the Russian campaign, chaplains and bishops in combat areas also wore an armband carrying a violet cross, but otherwise similar to the medical Red Cross armband. In combat areas outside Germany chaplains and bishops could also carry a pistol for self-protection but they did not, of course, normally bear arms.

Plate 168: *An Army chaplain taking a service in the field and wearing the chaplain's violet cross armband and vestments. Note the absence of shoulder straps.*

MEDICAL PERSONNEL

Army doctors and enlisted men in the medical services normally wore the internationally known 'serpent' cypher on their shoulder straps. In the field they also wore a Red Cross armband (red on white) on the left arm, and occasionally on both arms. This device was also worn by anyone else on medical duties such as stretcher bearers who might be drawn from non-medical units. In the campaign in Normandy in 1944, some stretcher bearers wore white overall vests showing a large Red Cross to both front and rear, as well as the red cross armband.

Plate 169: *A Feldwebel of the medical services attending to a wounded French soldier in June 1940 showing Red Cross armband and the serpent insignia on the shoulder strap.*

Plate 170: *An Unteroffizier acting as a stretcher bearer commander, wearing the Red Cross armband. The insignia on his shoulder strap is not the medical serpent but the 'L' of the 'Panzerlehr' demonstration battalion.*

169

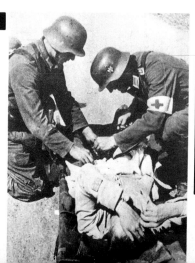

170

4. Collecting 'Das Heer' Material

Not everyone who is interested enough in aspects of World War 2 to read reference books about it is necessarily a collector of anything. However, almost everybody who finds a subject fascinating enough to want to find out more tends to look around to find what else is available to further the pursuit of the subject. This is certainly the case with military uniforms, insignia and equipment. Despite taking place around half a century ago, and beyond the memory of many people now alive, World War 2 in its many aspects is never far from the consciousness because there are still films, videos, TV presentations, books and magazines, not to mention scale models, appearing all the time covering World War 2-related subjects. There are museums, too, certainly in Britain and Western Europe, where World War 2 is covered and artifacts are displayed. If you want to pursue the subject, therefore, there are plenty of ways to do it.

UNIFORMS AND INSIGNIA

Undoubtedly the most desirable aim of the uniform enthusiast is to acquire actual examples of uniform items, badges and insignia from the World War 2 era itself. Today this is easier said than done, for the days when redundant uniform pieces could be picked up cheaply, or even for nothing, have long gone. The passage of time has seen to that. A lot of Third Reich material reached Britain and other West European countries in the immediate postwar period in the form of 'souvenirs' brought back by returning soldiers. There are still probably some pieces salted away in attics or boxrooms that have been there since 1945, and the lucky collector might come across these by word of mouth or through relatives, for example. This would be exceptional, however, and the only sure way today of acquiring original authentic uniform and insignia items is through the collectors' market. Even this is a largely uncharted area, for much of the business is done by specialist dealers who are known to the collecting fraternity but do not necessarily advertise to any great degree and may not even advertise at all.

However, if you want to make a start finding a specialist dealer a good place to look is in the classified advertisement section of as many local newspapers as you can find. You may draw a blank, but it is worth a look. Check out, also, the classified advertisement sections of military modelling and military interest magazines. Try also specialist classified advertisement journals such as Exchange & Mart.

Particular sources of specialist dealers are the local markets that concentrate on antiques. In most cases it is a matter of walking round and looking, for some of the booths are very small, tucked into corners. You will probably find badges and some items in quite a few antique markets, but not necessarily a specialist uniform dealer. Or you might find a uniform specialist who doesn't deal in the Third Reich era. In London there are two well-known street markets for antiques where there are dealers in uniform items who include Third Reich era material in what they have on offer. These are the Portobello Road W11 (between Notting Hill Gate and Ladbroke Grove) and Camden Passage N1 (near the Angel) street markets which operate on Saturdays and Sundays.

There are a few specialist dealers whose business has built up on a scale well beyond antique market level. One of the leading specialists is Malcolm Fisher whose large establishment, Regimentals, is at 70 Essex Road, Islington, London N1, not far from the Camden Passage street market. Regimentals has very large stocks of Third Reich material (and caters for some other eras as well, such as World War 1) and everything is authenticated and in good order. The company deals with collectors all over the world and issues regular catalogues of current stock which have, themselves, become collectors' pieces due to the excellent illustrations and descriptions contained therein. A mailing list service is available on application and opening hours are 10.00-17.00 daily except Sundays and Mondays. Visitors can therefore see everything well displayed. All the individual items of uniform and insignia illustrated in this book are from Regimentals' stock, just a small selection typical of what is available.

Though the stock is always changing, just about every item in the inventory of uniformed Third Reich organisations passes through and is recorded in the catalogue issues. A large percentage is of army uniforms and it would be possible to build up a good representative collection of Heer uniforms from this one source. Malcolm Fisher finds 'new' material from around the world all the time and an example of how this can happen half-a-century on from World War 2 is given by the recent acquisition of ex-World War 2 German uniform items which had been kept for film work by the costume department of a Russian movie studio — until Glasnost opened it up to the market in 1991.

The only thing that will hold back the keen uniform enthusiast is the cost of buying them! With scarcity and demand, prices have risen steadily over the years. For example, while it was possible to buy an ordinary 1935 pattern German steel helmet in 1973 for around £10, in 1993 £250 (UK) was a more typical price, with very much higher prices for rare or perfect examples. Some typical prices in 1993 were as follows:

• Army service tunic, 1936 pattern, with all insignia of rank and in good condition: £340
• Army service tunic, 1943 pattern, with all rank insignia, plus combat and campaign awards (Iron Cross 1st Class, Krim shield and in very good condition: £425
• 1943 Pattern Einheitsmütze (peaked forage cap), good condition: £115
• Infantry assault badge in bronze: £38
• Army close combat clasp ('Silver' Class), mint and unissued: £120
• The same item, worn: £90
• Afrika Korps cuff title: £35
• Army breast eagle, Bevo woven: £12
• Iron Cross 2nd Class, mint and unissued in original packet: £48
• Iron Cross 2nd Class, with ribbon, worn: £28
• MP40 sub-machine gun (deactivated): £325
• Army officer's parade dress trousers: £175
• Army leather marching boots, good condition: £100
• Belt hook for fitting to service tunic: £3 (each)

These are typical prices chosen from hundreds of items, but they give an idea of the sort of money a collector would need to purchase good quality items of Heer uniform, insignia and equipment today. It can be seen that anyone with a very limited budget might be restricted to collecting badges and insignia rather than clothing.

It must be said that the quality of the German military clothing was exceptionally good which has helped it to remain in good condition over a great length of time. The late war material is more skimpily made, but it is still well made by today's standards. Some items are scarce, even from specialist dealers. For example the 1944 pattern 'battle dress'-type blouse is quite rare. Beyond the specialist uniform and insignia dealer there are a few other ways of finding material on sale. The big auction houses sometimes include uniform and militaria sales in their schedules and usually produce catalogues (often well illustrated) in advance of sale day. It would be unusual to find a sale devoted only to Third Reich material, so the keen collector would need to peruse the sale catalogues to see what was included. Prices are rarely low at these sales, and rare pieces can bid high.

More modest prices might be found among uniform dealers who go to the various 'Aerojumble' and 'Militaria' days found at different venues during the year, most often at famous places where enthusiasts gather such as Brooklands, Tangmere, Yeovilton, Old Warden, and so on. For a modest admission charge the enthusiast gets access to numerous stands selling books, artifacts, relics, models, photographs and documents — and uniforms. Most of the uniform dealers have a mix of items among which there *may* well be Third Reich era material and it would be unusual at one of these events if nothing related to the German forces in World War 2 was to be found. There can be no precise price guidance and finding bargains is a matter of luck. But a very general observation concludes that at some Aerojumbles, items related to the German Army might be priced slightly lower than Luftwaffe items because most people attending are aviation fans and the dealer is concentrating on them.

If Third Reich era uniform items are acquired, the collector is better placed for conservation than with some other categories of uniform and equipment, due to the generally high quality of the materials used in manufacture. Unless there has been exceptional exposure to the elements, seams and sewing are likely to be sound and even fading is unsual to any great extent. But it is wise to keep uniform items out of direct sunlight or away from strong artificial light. How uniform items are displayed, however, is very much at the whim of the collector. Some will prefer to keep them in wardrobes, both for protection and to keep them from prying eyes in the event of burglary, etc. However, those who have a secure 'den' might prefer to display uniform items from rails, within glass cases, or on tailors' dummies, the latter being a most effective and dramatic form of display if complete uniforms and equipment sets are possessed. Many of the prime items in the Regimentals collection are displayed this way. Museums displaying clothing on dummies will give plenty of ideas for posing and positioning.

Malcolm Fisher, of Regimentals, who has many years experience of handling Third Reich era uniforms and equipment says that any uniform items in generally good condition on acquisition should need no more than an occasional moth spray, plus avoidance of sunlight etc, to keep them virtually indefinitely. If uniform items are being stowed away in wardrobes or cupboards for occasional inspection only, an obvious extra precaution is to use a cover of the type used by dry-cleaners. Malcolm Fisher says that dry cleaning itself is rarely necessary unless a uniform item is acquired in genuinely grubby condition. If buttons, shoulder straps or insignia are damaged or missing, it is generally possible to acquire individual replacements from dealers (even if it takes some time to locate a specific item), and this is often preferable to trying to repair embroidery or knock out dents, etc. All leather items benefit from a coating with Connolly hide food from time to time. Rubber is more of a problem as it can perish with time, but fortunately relatively few German uniform or equipment items include rubber.

Because of the high value of virtually all Third Reich items on the market, it is very desirable to insure your collection. There are no special deals available, or specialist uniform insurers, and the

Plate 171: *A PK-Berichter (Propaganda-Kompanie Reporter) types out his story near the frontline in the French campaign of June 1940. He wears the officer's old-style service cap and the narrow shoulder straps of Sonderführer.*

Plate 172: *A good example of a specialist badge on the cuff is shown on the Unteroffizier (left) who has the ordnance specialist badge. This vehicle is a French carrier captured in the fighting of May 1940 and is being used by an army unit.*

Plate 173: *An honour guard in 1939 wearing the prewar-style pointed shoulder straps and the field grey suede leather ribbed-back gloves.*

Plate 174: *The mortar crew of a demonstration battalion with the 'L' insignia on the shoulder strap. Note also the 'star' on the arm of an Oberschütze (right).*

Plate 175: *A general wearing a leather overcoat in field grey colouring.*

only sure way of insuring is to make an individual declaration and a collection, itemised in detail, and taking out a policy with any of the usual insurance companies or brokers.

Museums

Because Germany was the defeated nation there is no comprehensive collection of German World War 2 uniforms on display to the public in Germany – in other words no equivalent to the display of uniforms through the centuries (including World War 2) as is found in the British National Army Museum. Some regimental museums of the modern Bundesheer display uniforms of the World War 2 period alongside German uniforms of earlier periods but there is no location where there is a worthwhile display. Museums throughout Europe show examples of German World War 2 uniforms, and the most comprehensive display of all is the Third Reich Museum at Spa La Gleize in the Ardennes, a museum that otherwise largely commemorates the 'Battle of the Bulge'. The Bastogne Military Museum, also in the 'Battle of the Bulge' area, has a better than usual collection of German uniforms of World War 2. There are also German uniforms (and other equipment) to be seen at local museums in France, in particular at Dieppe, Arromanches (the D-Day Museum) and Bayeux. Many other military museums have representative German World War 2 uniforms and items of equipment, but there is no museum setting out to show all German uniform variations.

PRINTED EPHEMERA AND ARTIFACTS

The Aerojumble and Militaria events are also places where you might find all sorts of pieces at varied prices, and once again you can find some military items at Aerojumbles so do not exclude such events from your itinerary in the collecting quest. At these venues you might find models and kits, and you will certainly find books, old newspapers, old cuttings books, notices and paperwork, logbooks, paybooks, photographs, posters, vehicle badges and just about everything else you can think of. Typical interesting items are personal scrapbooks of snapshots and cuttings concerning a unit at war. Sometimes there are 'official' unit scrapbooks of this type, too.

The Third Reich made the fullest use of propaganda and publicity to keep the people informed and to promote the 'feel good' factor both among servicemen and the public in general. Weekly or monthly illustrated magazines with high standard of photography, layout and printing, often with some colour pages too, were published, and these can still be found. The most famous journal was *Signal*, produced in German, Dutch, French, Italian and English editions and containing military articles in virtually every issue. The armed forces had their own magazine *Die Wehrmacht* and every issue is of interest to collectors. These were official productions, but there were party-sponsored commercial magazines, too, most notably *Neue Illustrierte Zeitung* which included military coverage. Prices of these might be £3-£5 or more per issue, depending on the outlet. Less likely to be found are individual campaign books produced by various German military units. They are rarer and would cost more, but are worth looking for.

Any of the items noted here might be found with dealers as well as at sales of all sorts.

We might consider here photographs of the period. All the outlets already suggested might have photographs for sale, ranging from private snapshots taken by soldiers on campaign, to official or agency photographs of all sorts. There were also some propaganda and publicity postcards of photographic type issued in Germany during the Third Reich era. Millions of World War 2 photographs, including those covering German forces, are held in the photographic library of the Imperial War Museum, London SE1, and at the National Archives, Washington DC in the USA; these photographs can be ordered and purchased by members of the public. Another source of the official German war photographers' output is the photographic library of the Bundesarchiv, Koblenz, Germany, which is now open to the general public for bona fide research. Prints may be ordered and purchased from the millions of fine war photographs held in this official German government archive.

Also to be found are cards or prints depicting the work of official German war artists, either depicting individual soldiers or graphic action scenes, but these are much rarer than photographs.

Finally there are the modern books and magazines published since World War 2 covering uniforms, campaigns, military history, politics and much else relating to the German Army in the 1933-45 period. All can be collected to advantage by anyone interested in the subject and some old books are very inexpensive particularly if discovered at jumble sales.

Plate 176: *Publications for collectors: a copy of* Signal *and a very much rarer item, the highly detailed record of campaign published by 9th Army covering their part in the invasion of France in 1940.*

Plate 177: *Prints and postcards by official German war artists can sometimes be found, such as this print of a MG34 team in action on the Russian Front. The original is, of course, in colour.*

MODELS

Those who cannot afford actual items of Heer clothing and equipment — or who don't have room to store them — will find models very much cheaper! Not everyone is interested in model soldiers, but they offer a compact and interesting way of developing and displaying an interest in uniforms. A collection of model soldiers depicting every rank, order of dress and side arm of the 1933-45 Heer would be very spectacular indeed. Such a collection would take some time to build up or acquire, so a project of this type would be a very satisfying way of sustaining interest over a long period.

Military modelling is a big subject in its own right, but as far as models of German soldiers is concerned, the availability is good with more kits and models covering the subject than most. At the present time there are companies who will supply finished models to order, at a price, to anyone with no practical modelling ability. These firms advertise in the pages of *Military Modelling* magazine. Most of these figures are good quality metal to the standard 54mm (1:32 scale) size. Many of the metal figures are also sold more cheaply in kit form for home assembly. For the enthusiast with kit-building experience the hobby becomes very much cheaper. There are plastic kits featuring German soldiers from firms like Tamiya which require little more than assembling and painting, and the prices are at the low end of the scale. These plastic models can be altered and detailed to create variations of type, also. For example, heads and arms can be changed around among figures to give differing appearances. The Tamiya (and other Japanese-made) figures are to a slightly smaller scale of

Plate 178: *Among the cheapest models, highly accurate but needing painting, are the plastic sets in the Airfix range. This set of Mountain Troops is among several that Airfix produced.*

Plate 179: *Eight Afrika Korps figures in 1:35 scale can be assembled from a kit of plastic parts in the Tamiya range, one of several different German soldier sets they offer.*

ate 180: *A typical limited run 54mm (1:32 scale) ady-painted metal cast figure from one of the small ecialist suppliers. This is a Tambour-Major (Drum ajor) complete with 'Swallow's Nest' wings, one of a ole range of different German Army types produced ew years ago and now collectors' pieces in their vn right.*

1:35, through visually most of them mix well enough with the European 1:32 scale figures. In. these scales, too, are numerous vehicles, guns and tanks for those who want to make up scenic dioramas with the figures.

Beyond these popular and readily available scales are some larger scale models which make good display ornaments. There are also very small (1:76 scale or less) figures and vehicles for war games or large 'battle' dioramas.

Many of the 54mm scale models are made in short runs and are only on sale for limited periods. Thus they become collectors' pieces in their own right and could appreciate in value. We may associate with this some true collectors' pieces, namely model soldiers made in the Third Reich era. Britains, the famous British maker, only ever made one set in the late 1930s, No 432 German Infantry in their 'Armies of the World' series. This comprised an officer with sword and seven men marching 'at the slope' all in the 1936 pattern service dress and helmet. Today a boxed set would fetch a premium price at sale. Though Britains made many 'topical' British sets reflecting the 1939-40 events (eg, air raid wardens and AA guns), they did not make more German sets it seems before war conditions stopped production.

The classic Heer models of the Third Reich period were made in Germany, the two biggest makers being Elastolin-Haussmann and Lineol. All their models had great charm and character. They were made in a composition material and figures were about 60mm high. The ranges were most comprehensive and included all arms of the Wehrmacht as well as foreign types. Even some of the leading personalities of the time were modelled, including Goering and Hitler.

Though these are now all rare relics from the 1930s, it is a little-known fact that the Lineol moulds survived and these impressive models are available today from the present makers, Holz Modell Bau, Am Bahnhof 9, 4717 Nordkirchen 3-Capelle, Germany. An IRC sent to them will bring details. Apart from figures depicting all Heer branches, the range has tanks, vehicles and guns, all to scale and all in the prewar finish and markings.

MILITARY MUSIC

legitimate aspect of the collecting hobby, at ast with military subjects, would be recordings ' military band music. Over the years a fair umber of recordings of German Army marches ave been produced and some are always avail- ole, though most get deleted after a time. In Ger- any excellent recordings are available by mod- n Bundesheer bands and some of these are vailable in Britain and USA in shops which deal ith imports. Most the 'selections' tend to

include only the more famous marches such as 'Preussen Gloria' and 'Florentiner Marsch', but a now deleted series to look out for was a set called 'Traditionsmarsche' produced in the 1970s by Telefunken (Ref No: TS 3206/7/8) which took each region in turn and worked its way through all the military marches for each region, with the sleeve information relating the marches to the regiments that used them. This is definitely a set for the serious student of German military music.

Plate 181: *Two of the series of double-album Traditionsmärche sets by Telefunken which recorded the marches of all the German regiments.*

Plate 182: *Living history — a selection of prewar Lineol German Army figures which are still available from the original 1930s and 1940s moulds by a supplier in Germany.*

181

182

126

GLOSSARY OF UNIFORM TERMS

ENGLISH	GERMAN	REMARKS
Pack	Tornister	Canvas with leather binding
Tunic/blouse	Feldbluse	Service tunic
Trousers	Hosen	Service trousers
Greatcoat	Mantel	
Steel helmet	Stahlhelm	1943, 1935 or 1916 patterns
Field cap	Feldmütze	Fore-and-aft type forage cap
Mountain cap	Bergemutze	Peaked forage cap
Field cap (peaked)	Einheitsmutze	Derived from mountain cap — peaked
forage cap		
Tank helmet	Schutzmütze	Discarded in 1940
Peaked cap	Shirmmütze	Stiff peak cap
Tropical helmet	Tropische Kopfbedeckung	Pith helmet
Parade tunic	Waffenrock	
Swallow's Nest	Schwalbennesten	Bandsmen's 'wings'
Service dress	Dienstanzug	
Field dress	Feldanzug	Service dress worn with combat
equipment		
Parade dress	Paradenanzug	
Badge	Abzeichen	
Gorget plate	Ringkragen	
Marching boots	Marschstiefel	'Jackboots'
Riding boots	Reitstiefel	
Ankle boots	Schnürschuhe	
Mountain boots	Bergschuhe	Climbing boots
National insignia	Hoheitzabzeichen	Eagle emblem on breast
Rosette (caps)	Reischskokarde	
Shoulder straps	Schulterklappen	
arm of service colour	Waffenfarbe	
Belt	Koppel	
Decorative knot	Portepee, Troddel and Faustriemen	Carried on sword and dagger and bayonet hilts — parade dress
Braid	Litzen	
Collar patches	Kragenpatten	

127

BIBLIOGRAPHY

While very many books include illustrations of German soldiers, the following include actual detailed coverage, to a greater or lesser degree, of aspects of the uniform. Numerous books have been published covering German political and military history 1933-45.

John R. Angolia and Adolf Schlict, *Uniforms & Traditions of the German Army, 1933-45* (3 Vols) (R. James Bender Publishing, USA, 1984, 1986)
Very extensive coverage in great detail.

Brian L.Davis, *German Army Uniforms & Insignia 1933-45* (Arms & Armour Press 1971)
A very well detailed and highly illustrated single volume coverage.

Chris Ellis, *German Military Combat Dress, 1939-1945* (Almark Publications 1973)

Chris Ellis & Peter Chamberlain, *Gebirgsjäger, Afrika Korps, Panzer-Grenadiers* (3 Vols) (Almark Publications 1973)

German Military Police Units, the Panzer Divisions, German Commanders of World Wa (various authors) (Osprey Publishing 1975-9•

Handbook on German Army Identification (US Army 1943)

Handbook on German Military Forces (US Arm, eds 1941, 1943 and 1944)

Uniform source

Irrespective of other sources of uniforms a insignia for the collector, a major source authenticated uniforms and insignia of the G man Army (and other Third Reich uniforms) Regimentals, 70 Essex Road, Islington, Lond N1 8LT, England. The individual items shown this book are from Regimentals' stock. Regim• tals publishes a highly illustrated descriptive c alogue of stock from time to time, and these • themselves useful reference works.

Plate 183: *A German recce unit passes a knocked o (and obsolete) Russian armoured car during the advance into the Ukraine. This shows the front of th motorcyclist's rubberised coat and, in this case, the rifle slung across the chest.*